WILD HARVEST

Wild
HARVEST

AN ESSAY IN SELF-SUFFICIENCY

Hope L. Bourne

Illustrations by the author

EXMOOR
BOOKS

First published in 1978
Reprinted 2001, 2002 and 2015

ISBN 978 0 86183 431 0

British Library Cataloguing-in-Publication-Data
A CIP data for this book is available from the British Library

EXMOOR BOOKS
*Exmoor Books is a partnership between
Halsgrove and the Exmoor National Park*

Halsgrove House,
Ryelands Business Park,
Bagley Road, Wellington, Somerset TA21 9PZ
Tel: 01823 653777   Fax: 01823 216796
email: sales@halsgrove.com

Part of the Halsgrove group of companies
Information on all Halsgrove titles is available at:
www.halsgrove.com

Printed and bound in China by Everbest Printing Co Ltd

CONTENTS

Preface to Second Edition

THIS little book was written and first published some twenty-four years ago. Since then, much has changed, both in general affairs and in my own circumstances. There have been changes in matters of law, agriculture, currency and measurement, and I no longer live where I did.

However, I have preferred to leave the original text as it was then written rather than try and revise it. To attempt to alter one or two things would inevitably lead to altering more, and in no time the balance of words – and other things – would be disturbed.

All I will here explain is that in the days of which I write 20 shillings made the pound sterling, and 12 pennies went to the shilling. So from that you may calculate how much I had to live on – though it is to be remembered that the pound then went much further than it does today.

Beyond this, I leave the work as a 'period piece' of a time and a way of life that has passed.

H.L.B.
March 2001

In Search of Freedom

LONG ago – I can't remember now just how long ago in terms of the years of my life – I made up my mind that I would be independent, that I would live in as complete a state of freedom as was humanly possible, ordering my own affairs, making my own decisions, and being in all things my own master. I would live as I wished, not as other people thought I ought to, and in doing so I would not be beholden to the charity of the Welfare State.

Freedom: To stand upright before the world, to acknowledge no-one above one's head but God, to concede to no power except the Law of the Land. To inherit the earth and sky and the sun, the wind and the rain, and to be unconfined by walls except at one's own choosing. To freely say to the world whatever one had to say. This was the way of a free man, and it should be mine.

How was it to be accomplished, I having hardly any money in this world's terms, and little chance of getting more? Well now, how it was to be done, is set forth in this little book. Enough to say here, that I saw I must become selfsufficient, producing the basic necessities of life for myself as directly from Nature as I could. That I must either produce enough of the fruits of the earth to barter some for those commodities I could not provide for myself, or have some craft which I could sell to the same end. If I could do this, I could live.

Looking through and beyond the complex and tangled web of modern society to the roots of life, I saw that five things are necessary to human life – fresh water, food, fire, shelter and protective clothing. Given these, one can live. Without them, one will die. Of the five, the first two are absolutely essential to man and beast alike (for not even the lowest animal can exist without them) and the last three vital to man in a northern climate, though perhaps not quite so imperative in a tropical one. To live with *only* these things means a very harsh life, but at least one will not perish, and given this sound base to life one can hold on in hard times, and then when conditions are favourable, use this base as a foundation to build thereon a wider and wealthier life.

So, I must needs provide myself with these five essentials, or at least as much of each as I could, from the earth, by my own labour, with as little over head financial cost as possible.

Then being free, I could and would write. This for me would be at once a means of self-expression, a communication of thoughts and opinions, a congenial occupation, and ultimately (or so I hoped) the means of earning the little money I needed for such overheads as I would have to bear. In short, a vocation.

Thus I would have a free life, a way of life, one which would give me personal freedom and independence coupled with a vigourous outdoor life in the midst of the wild country I loved – the two things that matter most of all to me.

And the place in which to settle and grow roots like a plant? For me it must be a spot in wild untamed country, because therein is my heart. I love the wilderness (or what is left of it in this day and age). I love its space, its defiant freedom, its proud unconquered spirit, its wild and primal beauty, its challenge to the human soul.

So here I am as I have been for at least the last twenty-five years, tucked in a corner of one of the last remaining patches of wilderness-country in this South-West region of Britain. Of what those years have been to me, I now write.

H.L.B.
1977

CHAPTER ONE

Home

HERE I sit in all cosy and secure in my own little home this winter's night, with my writing-paper on my knee, my bright fire lighting its pages for me to write with my old familiar pencil.

Home! Oh how precious it is! How it encompasses me! Here is my stove with its flame-tongued logs cracking and murmuring, the singing kettle above, the jolly teapot in the hob below, iron frying pan and big boiling saucepan nearby, copper and brass reflecting the fiery glow. Here is my dresser-shelf with mug and jug and ready food, below it the cupboards filled with winter stores. There is my bunk-bed snug for me when I want it, there my shelves piled with books and working-stuffs. Everything here is dear and familiar, prized and precious, necessary for sustenance or else a small delight. Every single thing is a friend, old or new, known, a part of myself.

Beside me is the evening's pile of fuel – sawn logs – above me ticks the big-faced clock telling me the time, on the dresser-end the small oil-lamp glows, lighting my room and touching all my treasures as in an Aladdin's cave, and beside it sits my precious wireless set which brings all the world to me. A locker holds my guns (one of them at the moment lying on the top) and store of ammunition, my heavy sheathed hunting-knives hang in accustomed places. My prized deer-skins and others drape the bunks, slots, antlers and some favourite pictures fill the walls, thick-wooled sheepskins make warm the floor under my feet. A bridle hangs in one corner to remind me of the days when I possessed a horse, and near it a hunting-crop and pair of spurs. My trout-rod just manages to lie along one side of the little room and the old field-glasses in their battered leather case swing on a hook by the door. Books everywhere – big ones, little ones, old battered favourites, some small new ones (though I can scarcely afford to buy a book nowadays), all of them treasured, for books are the best of company. Papers and magazines, old in date but fresh in interest pile along the back of my bunk for bedtime reading. A calendar hangs above to mark the days. Bright tin boxes hold a variety of stuffs from things to eat to filed-away notes and sketches. Folios of paper and boxes of paints and pencils for work. Wads of letters from friends stuck behind clock and radio. Some precious and sentimental ornaments. A jar – or rather earthenware jug – of hazel-catkins and glossy green ivy-leaves by the window. A jug and bucket of fresh water by the door. All these and so many smaller things – all and each a part of my life, vital to body or soul or both, the whole of which make Home.

This for me is home all in one small space, and here am I in its nutshell of life, whilst outside rain lashes out of the blackness of night and a rising storm shakes the trees and sends its roaring voice across the moor and down the combe. All around, mile upon mile of hill and bog, field and wood and stream-filled valley lie in the dark, hidden from me but felt intensely like a Presence. Far-off, each a mile or so in distance at the nearest, lie hill-farms, islands of light and life in the immensity of winter night, and each is a neighbour, unseen now but known.

Nearer, girded about me, is my little garden, sleeping in the darkness with its lawn and pretty plants to flower in the summer. Behind is the barn full of hay, to left and right a lean-to and small shed, each holding garden-tools and the general overflow from this, my caravan home. 'Over the way' lies my high- banked vegetable garden, backed by the shippon-range of old buildings, tallets likewise stuffed with hay under dripping eaves.

Beyond the gates the lane begins, starting on its outward journey to civilization – or what passes for that in these parts. Rough and stony and grass-matted in the middle, pooled with mud in parts, it goes down a quarter-mile to a gate and little bridge over a rushing moorland stream. Thence it debouches onto the open moor for a mile, becoming a track amongst bracken and rushes, rainwashed and rutty. Eventually it reaches a tarmaced road and ends thereat, having made contact with the twentieth century. (A further three miles will land one in the little village which is the metropolis for these parts.)

So here I am, snug and safe in my own little nutshell of life, all personal comforts to hand, surrounded without by a world of grandeur, beauty and freedom, far off from all the ugliness and suffocating confinement of urban industrial complexity, myself master of my own life.

Oh what a precious thing is home, be it what it will or where it is! Next after life itself, it is the most vital thing in human – and indeed animal – existence. To the baron his castle, to the peasant his cottage, to the bird its nest, to the rabbit its burrow. The horse looks to its stable, sheep and cattle have their learing-places. Even the fierce beasts have their lairs and deer their harbour. Ducks and hens come to their roost at dusk. The nomad comes home to his tent, and to the pig its sty is dear.

Home! After the immediate bodily necessities of brute creation, it is truly the most vital of needs. It is the rooting of life in the immensity of the Universe, the beginning of identity. It is stability in the midst of complexity, security in the face of uncertainty. It is the place from which your go forth and to which you return. It is shelter from the elements, the place of rest. It is the place where a family is raised and friends entertained, yet where comfort in loneliness and sorrow is found. It is the place to which you bring the spoils of life and wherein you display your treasures. It is the place that is your own tiny kingdom, whereof you are sovereign lord. For, saith the man of law (Coke), 'a man's house in his castle, *et domus sua cuique est tufissimum refugium*; for where shall a man be safe, if it be not in his own home?' Home is both earthly root and the extension of personality. It is also the beginning of independence, for in another's house you cannot be free. It is better to be in one's own home, be it only a tent or shack with a strawed floor than to share another's house in utmost luxury.

Home! It is the place one's heart longs for after absence, the thought of which causes your heart to tighten as you turn your footsteps thither. How one's eyes seek for the first glimpse, the familiar gable, as you return from a long journey in foreign parts!

So I have my own precious little home. It is the thing I have fought to obtain and to keep all my life. Before this tiny place in which I now live and write and have my being, I have had others and called many places home. All but one have been in spots as wild, or almost so, as this, for I love the wilderness with a deep and positive love. For me, the wild places are space and freedom, the space to be myself, the freedom to live as I like to live and to do the things I like to do. To shoot, to fish, to garden, to write, to paint, to walk, to ride (though I do not at present possess a horse) and to hunt (which I do on foot). To live with Nature in its beauty and grandeur and to accept the challenge of its might.

Home is dear wherever it may be, but no-where more so than in a wild and lonely place. Here in the face of Nature home is the precious focal point offering life where otherwise there would be none. Here is shelter from the storm, hot food and dry clothes after hours in the rain, a bright fire and a cosy bed on a winter's night, lamplight in the darkness. Here all my treasures wait for me, here is comfort, security, rest after the day's adventuring.

To make a home in the wilderness is in itself an adventure. Whether it is the rehabilitation of an ancient cottage or the settling of a caravan on a fresh patch, or even the putting-up of a tent in a wild spot, it is an essay in pioneering in some sort. Everything has to be brought, hauled or carried, usually over rough terrain, and one has to begin with the barest essentials. Starting with the vital necessities of a sound roof against inclement weather, a fire and a water supply, and progressing from store-foods to the establishment of a garden and fresh vegetables, then gradually to such refinements and such small luxuries as round-off a contented life, one shares adventure once more with the early settlers and pioneers, and the world becomes young again.

How exciting it is to come to a place and make it home! I remember my coming here seven long years ago – bringing up the first necessities of life in a rucksack, getting Land-Rover lifts for the heavier things I couldn't carry, doing emergency repairs to keep the rain from coming through the roof, fencing the garden-patch, and exploring all the nooks of the surrounding countryside. This precious place growing into Home, each small thing becoming as another staple in the framework of the whole, each small act binding me to it and it to me, until I could say to anything, plant or object, brought hither 'Welcome home!' So a home grows, moulded around one, perhaps the most wonderful of all creative achievements.

So much one learns – not only of practical things, and constructional matters, but of true values and the simplicity of real comforts and pleasures. What is luxury? As understood in modern terms it is (to me) something largely superfluous, nice to have if you have a taste for it and can afford it, but not necessary to real happiness. One of the great misconceptions of the present day is that a simple or primitive life is a deprived and uncomfortable life. Nothing can be further from the truth.

4

A log-fire is the most joyful of all forms of heating. Food cooked on it has a flavour unmatched by any other means. The soft glow of an oil-lamp or just the flickering firelight is kinder to the eyes and more pleasing to a room than the hideous glare of an overpowering centre-ceiling electric light. A mattress stuffed with hay or springy rushes is more comfortable than the most expensive sprung-bed. It is more cosy to recline in a be-rugged bunk by a fire than to sit upright on a chair in a stifling centrally-heated room. Sheep-skins make deeper warmer floorcovering than pile-carpets. Food fresh from the garden tastes incomparably nicer than that out of tins, packages and 'fridges. Wild meat got by hunting is richer and stronger than anything out of a butcher's shop. Water from a spring is sweeter than that from a pipe. One gallon of water poured over oneself in a shower is more refreshing and hygienic than a soak-bath in fifty gallons. Add to all this the greater vigour and health gained by such a life, and the zest for enjoyment of all things that comes from it, the delight of looking on and living in the midst of a beautiful landscape, and here is true wealth.

Yes, to be here this night in comfort and cosyness, secure from the driving rain and the blackness of a winter's night, surrounded by my small treasures and pleasures, able to do whatever I wish within this small space of being, is of itself *real* luxury. Such are true values.

This past afternoon I struggled home across the moor in the teeth of driving, blinding rain, so hard that it stung like shot and so cold it numbed my face and hands, bent head-down to bore into the wind that battered me so that I could scarcely keep my footing stumbling amongst the stones and splashing pools of the track. Soaked at every point, and nightfall coming on, with what thankfulness I heard the roaring of the river that proclaimed the little bridge and gate to the lane – a first Amen as my hand groped for the hasp! Now half-shelter from the hedge, now the last effort up the lane, feet slipping in the mud. Darkness taking hold now, but every step a step towards Home. Oh the things I promise myself – dry clothes, hot tea, hot supper, bright fire to read my letters by (those letters held in the one waterproof part of my satchel). Now I am at the garden gate, now my wet fingers fumble with the door of my tiny dwelling – and I am Home – Amen seven times over!

H . L .

CHAPTER TWO

Economics and Economies

ECONOMICS are a hard fact of life, but there are economics and economics, and mine are somewhat different to other people's.

Most people equate economics with money and money alone. Now, as I have probably said elsewhere, I do not. I long ago tumbled to the fact that money is not a thing in itself, but a symbol of other things. Money as such is of value only for what it can be exchanged for. Therefore the reality is more important than the symbol.

So many folk beggar themselves and ruin their lives for money. 'Tis said, a man without money may be poor, but he that has nothing but money is poorest of all. How true this is. Whilst a certain amount of money is necessary for commerce and viability in a modern society, to make it the criterion of all one does in life and the accumulation of it an aim and end in itself is a folly of false standards. To do so is to make a slave of yourself, with money your master.

Long past, I made up my mind that I would never set out to make money as such, that I would not do anything specifically for the gain of money. I would do what I believed was right for me to do, right under my particular circumstances, the best thing I could do in life with what talents I had, and I would hope that money, enough for my needs, would come from this. Such has been my philosophy, and so far it has not let me down.

Earlier in this little book I think I have said that the essential, physical, needs of life are five – to wit, home, fire, water, food and winter clothing – and therefore the best and soundest economy for one with very little money is to obtain and produce these, or as much of each of these as you can, direct from Nature by your own labour. Therein lies stability and independence. Having these basic elements of life, you cannot be 'starved into submission' as can those who must have cash for *everything* they need. Next, you need to draw in from whatever is your chosen work a *little* money with which to buy those things which you cannot produce for yourself. Or, to barter surplus natural produce for said other things.

For me, the basis of all sound economics is, never buy what you can get for nothing (that is, produce for yourself). Don't borrow. Don't get into debt. Keep your overheads as low as possible until you are sure of sustaining them. If you can't afford a thing go without till you can. When you *have* got money, spend it wisely, on whatever is a good investment for life.

Also, keep your equipment at the simplest level, avoiding as far as possible anything that is likely to go wrong and need specialist attention. The last is always expensive, and often hard to get far out in the country. The simpler your gear is, the less there is to go wrong with it, and if and when it does, then you can mend or repair it yourself, which doesn't cost anything.

Ability to produce my own basic necessities and to do my own running repairs is the cornerstone of my economy. Truly the more primitive one's life is under wilderness conditions, the more satisfactory it is because there is nothing much to go wrong. Of everything here about me, there's only one thing that I could not myself repair if it went amiss, and that's my radio set – and that of course is a luxury.

This brings me to certain facts of self-sufficiency. Having by some means acquired a home – be it a caravan or a tumble-down cottage – the first thing to see that you have is, if not a hearth, a wood-burning stove. Stoves are not hard to come by, as stupid folk chuck them out in favour of gas, electricity, etc. I have three, one in the caravan, one in the shed, and one in the lean-to – two of them were rescued from dumps. There's always wood of some sort in the country, and just a handful of sticks will give you a hot meal at no cost at all. (It is true I have a small quick-cup-of-tea oil stove, but like the radio it is a luxury and I'm not dependent on it.)

Water can be taken for granted here in the hills, since there are springs everywhere, and in a country of high rainfall there's always rainwater. If you have a roof you can always arrange some catchment from it. Some sort of water-butts are necessary – just a couple of big buckets will do – two, so that one can be cleaned whilst the other is filling. (And the great thing about not having plumbing is that there's nothing to freeze-up and burst in icy weather.) Rain-water is always soft and sweet both to drink and to use – well, maybe the roof isn't scrubbed, but as they say in Australia, you've got a choice between dead bird (rainwater) or dead sheep (creekwater) so take your pick. I never saw a sick Australian in the back-country.

Then to establish a garden. This for me is the root of my existence. Now many folk setting out to be self-sufficient tend to make one initial blunder. They invest in livestock before they either know how to deal with such, or are aware of the fact that domestic animals have to be fed. Poultry with a view to eggs, goats or a cow for milk. Now this is a bad essay in home-economy for the hard-up or the inexperienced. All farm creatures have to be hand-fed in the winter, and you either have to produce the food for them before you produce it for yourself or buy it – and stock-feed costs money! – and in the latter case you may find you are spending more on the creatures than you are getting back, so to speak. Also, in the case of the larger animals you may have illness or accident, there will be vet's bills (which are very heavy) and in the end something may die on you, which in the case of a cow is a very big loss to sustain. It is much better to establish a good garden, off which you can produce almost all the food you need and then, for meat, invest in a good gun and persuade your farmer-neighbours to let you shoot rabbits and woodpigeons.

Re the latter, I am all for the conservation and cropping of wild-life. It costs nothing to keep, looks after itself, and provides sport as well as good food. Domestic stock should come at the end of the chain of self-sufficiency. Unless and until you have plenty of pasture or a sure surplus of home-grown vegetables it is not wise to sink your savings in such. But when conditions do permit, then get sorts closest to the wild and small in stature – the double reason for this is, breeds that are not over-specialized are likely to be healthier, and those that are small-bodied are in better balance with Nature's own economy and handier in carcass-size for home-killing and eating.

Of gardening, there's a chapter to come, so all I'll say here, what one patch of earth, lovingly cultivated, will give you of fresh food, good health and personal joy, is one of life's miracles. Just a square yard of fertile soil is the most precious thing in the world, did Man but realize it. My little garden of four square rods virtually keeps me. A quarter-acre would keep a family in basic food, i.e. fruit and vegetables. A full acre will yield from ten to twenty tons of good food, according to sorts of soil and methods of cultivation, enough to provide a family of five or six with all the vegetable-food they can eat, and support of its surplus some animals for meat and dairy-produce. But modern man does not value the precious soil – he thinks food grows on shop-shelves and land exists only as space to cover with concrete and tarmac.

Which brings me to the economics of a balanced life versus waste. Most of the imbalance of modern life is due to the threefold evil of greed, laziness and waste. The last prevails everywhere. All around outside of my little world I see it. Waste of water in heedless gallons for needless purposes (then the cry for new reservoirs to flood fine valleys when waste has drained the present ones dry). Waste of ground, that would grow good food, as patches of nettles around homesteads and small-town factories alike (cry for higher wages to buy processed food). Waste of food itself (how much gets spoilt and thrown away). Waste of good manure, by-products from farm, garden and household channeled away as refuse (so buy expensive fertilizer if you cultivate land at all). Waste of clothing – throw it out barely used because it's out of fashion in six months time (more wage-demands because folk say they can't clothe themselves). Waste of all other things – don't repair any object, just throw it away and buy another (more money wanted).

Yes, but, you may say, all this is good for trade and employment. Possibly, but it all comes back to the land. The more you waste, the more you want, the more natural resources you use up, the more life-giving land you destroy to make sites for industrial plants, and then there's less good soil to grow food and provide the other basic necessities of life. So goes the vicious circle.

Now for myself I dare to say I have evolved a way of life and an economy in which there is virtually no waste. Producing almost all my own food (the only regular thing I buy is a loaf of wholemeal bread per week, whilst the extra stores I lay in for the winter are simple things like oatmeal, nuts and dried fruit). I neither take material from the earth in the form of tins or plastic nor clutter-up the countryside with them. Of the very few cans I do get (which stuff may be given me as Christmas presents by friends) the larger continue a useful life as flowerpots, whilst the smaller do duty for target-practice. All refuse from household and garden and from about the old farm I compost, turning it into a rich and wholesome manure for the garden. I burn wood for fuel (which is a renewable resource) and the ash I save in bags for top-dressing the garden in Spring. So I don't have to buy fertilizer – or worry about sewage or dustbin-collection. Since I have to carry water buckets, I don't waste that either – so I don't have to deplete the water-supply.

Other economics for living involve a lot of make-do-and-mend, from clothes to household goods. Clothing would be an expensive item if I bought it new, but I don't: I have found it amazing what good stuff you can pick up at jumble-sales, almost new, some of it for a few pence. Almost anything comes in handy, and I can do a useful job with needle and thread in the winter evenings. All household articles I try to mend before resigning myself to taking money out of the bank for new.

As for what can be had for nothing, it is remarkable what can and to what uses the stuff can be put. (It's also remarkable what a lot of storage-space you need to be really self-sufficient – once you start stock-piling both essentials of life and useful rubbish, you find that out with a vengeance.)

Things that come under the heading of useful junk are cord off hay and straw bales (immensely strong stuff this, serving a dozen purposes about a homestead), sheep-cake and fertilizer-bags (the latter make first class waterproof coverings for anything), old broken-bottomed buckets, pans and bowls for plant-tubs, bits of plank for constructional purposes, lengths of wire, wooden boxes for seed-trays, cardboard boxes for God-knows-what, bits of metal that might come in useful for this-and-that, and, oh, all sorts of anything that just *might* come in useful. Usually they do – it's truly said, if you keep a thing for seven years you find a use for it!

Now there's another economy to be considered. This is economy of time. Time is an important factor of life, perhaps the greatest, since it is limited to twenty-four hours a day, and the days of one's life are not without end. It may be justly said, it is worth while spending money in order to save time on minor matters. True, if you have the money in the first place. But, if in order to get money you have to give up time doing what you don't want to do, then the argument breaks down. In the end it boils down to the choice of spending your time in ways that your either like or don't like. Myself, I find pleasant all the simple chores that I do for myself, and as for the time taken by them – as away from more creative and progressive pursuits – I find this little if daily management is good. As, for instance, with a properly-run garden I find an average of an hour a day will produce for me all the fruit and vegetables I need. (How much time one spends in a flower-garden doesn't count, since this is something one does for pure pleasure.)

Lastly, there is the money-economy of the returns from writing, etc., and the saving or spending thereof. Writing, as everybody knows (or perhaps not everybody *does* know) is the most uncertain, precarious and poorly-paid trade in the world, to be essayed only as a vocation. Looking back over the years of what may be called my 'working life' I think it is fair to say that my income 'from all sources' has averaged out at about £100 per annum. Of course in good years it has been more – I think about £300 is the most I've had in one year – but set against this is the fact that it has sometimes been less than £25. Yet not only have I always managed, evening-out the good against the lean, but I've been able to save the half of what I've earned overall. That is to say, of £100 I've been able to save £50 since £50 has been quite enough to live on. This last has worked out at about £12 for my regular weekly small loaf, box of matches and a postage stamp (approx. 4 shillings and 8 pence per week), £20 for all extras as they come up – ammunition for the rifle, wireless batteries, seeds for the garden, paint for the caravan, paper to write and draw on, jumble-sale bargains, etc., plus the odd small luxury like a piece of chocolate when there's a few pennies over, £18 for winter stores – paraffin, oatmeal, tea, etc., which in fact usually last me the rest of the year.

Such is my economy, and on this I maintain independence and health, and furthermore, in all this while I have never begged, never borrowed, never owed money – and that's more than the Chancellor of the Exchequer can say!

CHAPTER THREE

Practical Prairie-Busting

HERE I stand in the sunshine and look round on my little kingdom. A tiny home, a toolshed, a lean-to serving many purposes, a flower-garden and a vegetable garden strongly fenced. Encircling, beyond my defences, the wild land presses close and looks in at me, its tangle of bracken and bent, rush, gorse, brambles and heather ever ready to re-possess my holding.

Seven long years ago I came here to an overgrown thicket of rank grass and scrub, long abandoned and broken-fenced, then with hard labour transformed it into a little world of my own. How precious it now is and how I love it!

Now, I have been asked more than once by friends less used to dealing with Nature-in-the-Raw, how does one set about tackling such a job in the first place? Well, firstly, this battle, this struggle for a home and a garden in a place such as this, could not have been fought and won without those most necessary allies, good tools.

One of the things that has set Man above the animal kingdom is his ability to make and use tools. Tools, the best one can get, are a priority, and if one does not possess them at the start of a venture, they must be acquired. They must be saved-for, purchased with whatever money one may have, whenever one has it, all other desirable things being set aside, until a proper equipment is attained. Your well being, maybe your life, depends on them.

For me, my tools here reposing in the shed, are precious and vital things. Precious because each one represents a carefully considered personal choice, a struggled-for investment at some point in a lifetime, vital because even now I could scarcely hold my own here in the wilderness without any one of them.

Here they are, each set in its appointed place, each having done good yeoman service for me, and ready to hand when wanted again. In what order should I enumerate them? First I think the heavy claw-headed hammer and the bow-saw. (Once you have these you do can running-repairs to your home and also saw wood for a fire and for fencing.) Then my trusty digger or mattock. This, with its powerful steel head and axe-like spur set at rightangles, is the most versatile of all farm-and-garden implements. It can be used for nearly everything: for grubbing-up tree-stumps, for digging, for hoeing. Swung with full force it will go through almost anything. With this one tool you can clear and break rough scrubby ground and till a garden.

Coming next after the digger as an essential of life is the crow-bar. This elemental tool serves a variety of purposes. From the bashing in of fencing stakes to the raising and lifting of weights heavier than oneself and beyond one's capacity of direct lifting. Together with the bar goes a rope with a breaking-strain of not less than 1000 lb. (Remember, these two simple things – the rope and the lever – raised Stonehenge, and what can be accomplished with them by one person having knowledge of simple mechanics is remarkable!)

Further pioneering tools are a billhook or hedge-chopper for limbing-out, a staff-hook or hedge-slasher for clearing brambles and thistles, and a longtailed fork (or muck-fork as it is commonly called) for clearing-up.

Then specifically garden tools: a good digging-spade and fork, each with a length of blade and tines of about a foot. A rake with long teeth for deep working. A hoe of strong swan-necked 'field' pattern (weeds tend to be big and tough in these parts). A pair of strong shears, and lastly a trowel and small hand-fork.

In the farther lean-to repose a ladder and a wheel-barrow. The ladder is a shortish stout wooden one, of just the height necessary for getting up onto shed roofs or reaching lower tree-branches for lopping off. The wheelbarrow is a light but strong metal one, a most versatile thing, not specifically for garden use but as a general transport vehicle. It is amazing what you can shift over a considerable distance with a wheelbarrow!

Oh yes, and a wood-trolley, constructed for me by a friend from some boards and four old pram-wheels – very useful.

Something else too, home-made from two hessian sacks split and sewn together, is a carrying-sheet on which I can lump as much of anything as I can hump on my shoulders. (In certain situations, i.e. very rough or steep ground, this is actually more useful than a wheeled contrivance.)

Other useful things around are old buckets (also for carrying things), marking-strings for making straight lines, and a throwing-stone – a stone tied to a length of cord for throwing over high branches to pull them down to lopping-level.

To return to smaller refinements, the pair of powerful pliers, wire-cutters, screwdrivers and chisels are desirable for a variety of jobs inside and out. Knives, the first requisite of a pioneer life, can be taken for granted.

Then the work remembered! I have come to many places and had to start from scratch to create either a home or a garden or both, and I have learned the hard way how best to set about it. First of all, the very first thing I've always tried to do is to make my home water-tight and see that I have a fire. If the roof is leaking badly, then at least I've tried to repair that part nearest the hearth or stove. The quickest expedient, I've found, is to get a 'sheet' over it – if one possesses a sheet. Now ricksheets or tent fly-sheets, whether of tarpaulin or modern nylon-plastic, are expensive, but if finances will run to it a strong one of reasonable size – say 10 ft. x 15 ft. – is a good investment, for sooner or later you will need it when part of a roof blows off. If not, then for temporary repairs split fertilizer bags, which are of tough waterproof plastic (and can usually be had for nothing) I've found to be a good substitute – each will cover an area of about one square yard. Thus there's one dry cosy corner in which to sleep and have hot food and be comfortable, and this is a vital thing in more than the plainly practical sense: it is the beginning of Home, the base of operations from which everything else is conducted.

The next thing – fences, barriers, boundaries. Until you can fence-out the beasts of moor and field you cannot make a start on gardening or anything else or safeguard anything outside of your own four walls. So the first step of the would-be pioneer is the erecting of stockproof fences. This in itself is a major undertaking for the beasts of the moor are rapacious, cunning and persistent. The first requisite is barbed wire and stakes, supplemented by whatever other sorts of wire you can get, from pig-wire to wire-netting. Now all this is expensive if you buy it new, but generally speaking there is no need to do so. Farm rubbish-dumps are hives of such stuffs in various odd lengths, and my neighbours have always been quite pleased to let me take any of it away. There is of course the problem of getting it home from a distance of a mile or two away, but it is surprising how great a weight you can carry on your shoulders once you are used to it. (And its amazing too how great a weight a roll of wire-netting can be!)

Stakes can be cut-out from hedge-timber. Ash is the best of what is usually available, oak or chestnut good, if you can get it. These do not rot in the ground, at least not for a long while. Beech is virtually useless for any outdoor construction as it deteriorates very quickly, and is to be used only for temporary stop-gaps. Withy does quite well – and sometimes sprouts into a hedge of itself! Larch makes good rails. Sycamore is also useful.

The act of putting up a fence is more than a material one – it is an establishment of self and territory. It proclaims your presence and your right to be *here*. The line of it is as the frontier to other forces often to be warred with. Here inside is security for precious plants and all else that matters to you, beyond the barrier wild Nature holds away with all its legions.

But back to practical matters. A stock-proof fence needs to be just that – strong enough and high enough to hold back cattle, ponies, sheep and deer, and proof against rabbits and hares. Since effective fencing needs to be at least four feet high, stakes must be five feet to allow one foot in the ground, and wire-mesh 3' 6" topped with a line of barbed wire. To be rabbit-proofed wirenetting should be of 1½" mesh and the bottom of it buried in the ground, weighted under big stones, or pegged-down with small stakes (even then one will have to constantly inspect it to make sure some beastly bunny is not burrowing under).

Hours of hard work wielding the heavy bar, driving and hammering, struggling with rolls of mesh, cursing and wrestling with barbed-wire (barbed wire is one of the most vicious things ever invented by Man, but absolutely necessary to this job as it is the only thing cattle respect) then it is done, and one can survey the results of one's labours with pride and consider oneself now firmly entrenched. Such a feeling of satisfaction!

Oh, and a gate. An important thing this, and again so much more than a necessity. A gate is the entry into the estate, the stronghold. Pass through it and your are either leaving your secure territory for the wilds of life, adventure-bound, or you are returning home, coming back to the haven of your very own place. (In the days of great estates and grand houses, the main gates with their lodges were, significantly, works of architecture and fine craftsmanship, their heraldic devices proclaiming the pride of family possession. Earlier still, the gatehouse of the castle was its strongest point of outer defence.) So, the simplest gate is a thing of meaning. If I were rich I would have a fine one, but since I am not, and even field and garden gates when new cost more than I can afford, I have to make-do with old repaired ones or just home-made ones.

A simple gate is not difficult to make if one has some lengths of suitable timber – the best are bits of old shuttles of broken discarded farm gates which so often lean in hedges doing nothing – and can get a couple of old hinges and hangers from somewhere. But it must be strong – remember the castle gate leads into the stronghold! – and it must always be kept shut and hasped.

Having secured my territory, my next step has been to clear the ground. As I have already made plain, it is the nature of this wild country to be rockstrewn and scrub-covered, and if you come to a place either long-abandoned, or one where you have to break virgin soil for a garden, then you have to take the land like a pioneer.

First, slash down all the brambles, gorse and wild weeds – then you can see about you. Now look critically at what timber there may be. Stand in your patch and look in the direction of the prevailing wind and consider if some of the standing timber might not best be left as a windbreak. Consider also if one or two shapely young trees might well stay as ornamental things. In both cases, consider well, for often you will have to decide between the relative virtues of windbreak, aesthetic pleasure and sunlight. The timber that will protect your home and garden may also keep the sunshine out, and nothing will thrive in heavy shade. The final decision must be a careful one, one factor being balanced against another, and the fact being remembered that once you have felled a tree you cannot put it back, nor grow another like it for many years.

The wind is here a mighty force, its winter gales lashing the land with ruthless ferocity, and shelter is vital for man, beast, and plant alike. The higher farmsteads all have planted windbreaks of beech and sycamore about them. No-one but a fool cuts down timber that is holding back the wind. I once made that mistake, getting down an over-grown beech hedge that was keeping the morning sunshine off my patch. Oh dear, I may have got the sun in but I also got the east wind which absolutely flayed everything in the garden. Since then I have struggled to plant young saplings of ash, sycamore and poplar (the latter very quick-growing) as replacements on the outside of the hedge, but it will be many years before I have a really effective windbreak again. The lesson is driven well home – timber that takes twenty minutes to cut down cannot be replaced under twenty years – so think carefully first!

Getting down small timber is easy enough, but if it is anything bigger than the thickness of your leg, be careful. The weight of standing timber is always great, its spread bigger than you think, its fall not always predictable. Don't start on it until you are quite sure you know what you are doing.

One of the best ways of dealing with something biggish is to first lop the branches then halve the trunk, then saw-off at ground-level. By this means there is less to cope with – and less to fall on you – at any one stage.

Having got timber down, the next step is to clear up the mess. It's a matter of limbing-out any wood worth keeping for logs or poles and standing it up out of the way, then faggoting the rest and stacking the faggots likewise. (Burning-up right beside a homestead I don't like - it is too risky – just one spark blown into a hay-strewn shippon or up under old dry-raftered eaves, and it's too late to wish you hadn't started a fire in the first place.)

Next comes the task of shifting other debris off the land: if the patch is one which was *once* a garden long ago, then the odds are that you will have to delve out, gather-up and generally remove all manner of old cans, bits of bedsteads, and even parts of antiquated agricultural machinery (how such stuff ever got into a garden in the first place, I can't think) to say nothing of quantities of broken glass (what does one *do* with it? – well, dig a deep hole and bury it if you can; if the soil isn't deep enough take the line of least resistance and dump it out of sight behind a wall somewhere); If on the other hand you are dealing with 'virgin' ground, then most likely you will have some big stones or boulders to shift. If these are too heavy for direct lifting, the crow-bar and rope will shift them for you. Later you can probably use them for some ornamental feature. Then, if you have had to fell saplings on the garden-patch-to-be, there will be the roots to move. The best way to shift tree-stumps is to grub around them with the digger, saw through each root as you come to it, then finally heave the boles out with the bar.

Now to the final act of breaking the ground itself for cultivation. This is a job best done in winter, when the frosts have bitten down all top-growth. Here the digger comes into its own, smashing its way through couch-grass, nettle-roots, litter of brambles and gorse. An hour or so of vigorous work each cold short winter's day, and by early spring the earth is ready for the forking-out of the coarse stuff for the base of the first compost heap, and the final digging or 'tilling' for the first crop. So is a home established, and a garden made out of a wilderness.

H.L.B.

CHAPTER FOUR

Fire on the Hearth

OF all the things within a home, of all the blessings bestowed on Mankind above the gifts to the beasts, that of fire is surely the greatest or one of the greatest. Man alone can create fire and control it, and by this is lifted up to an existence above the animal kingdom.

Fire on the hearth! It is man's oldest ally in the struggle for life. The wonderful thing, the mighty power, the inexplicable element, that consents to come into our human lives, to live upon our hearths, life-giving with its fierce heat in the bitter cold of winter, lighting the darkness with its marvel of flame, giving hot food and comfort, drawing folk in company to its warmth, a fellowship to the lonely, repeller of wild beasts of the night and the evil spirits of men's minds. Little wonder that Man in ancient times worshipped fire, set an altar for it, and held it manifestation of god-like power and symbol of purity.

Through all the ages the fire on the hearth has been the heart, the core of the household. The hearth itself has been called the Altar of the Home: enter a room, and your eyes go instinctively to the fireplace and you move towards it. You sit with your friends around it, talk by its flames, think your thoughts by its glowing embers. To tend a fire, to light it, you kneel before it – this is imposed by the nature of things, but it is also symbolic. Fire has given Man true home, for home is where the hearth is.

I have had many fires and fireplaces in my wilderness-life, from a great open hearth to a succession of wood-burning stoves, and each for me has been the core of my home, my sustainer of life, my companion of the winter nights. Oh, the joy of a bright fire in the gathering dusk, the drying warmth of it when you come in from the rain of a soaking wet day, the leaping flames of it when frost and ice bind the darkness without! Oh, the comfort of singing kettle and sizzling frying-pan!

The wonderful companionship of it: for the living fire is a Presence, filling the room with light and life. Its leaping flame, its glowing caverns and fissures of furnace red, its hot breath, its crackle and movement, its waxing and waining, is a company of life to life. Come into a room in which there is a fire, and there is a comrade and a welcome; enter the same room when there is no fire, and there is emptiness and a lack of life. He who has fire is never lonely, though alone in the human context, for he has the Presence of the Fire before him and all about him.

It is of course the real fire, the wood-fire of which I speak, for there is none other that is a true fire. It is the joyous fire of crackling flame and fierce heat, of sweet-scented soft blue wood-smoke that creeps like incense down the twilight combes, of hot savoury food, of the singing kettle on the job. No other fire of any sort is there to match it for joy. Coal is foul-smelling, gas and electricity, though convenient for the housewife, are lifeless and soulless, and paraffin is an abomination except for lamp-lighting. The log fire is the fire of magic and delight. Also, it is the fire whose fuel is to be had direct from Nature, for wood, per trees, is a renewable resource in the ecological scheme of things. The burning of it too, gives a residue of precious ash, rich potassium, which serves as fine fertilizer for the garden, also a dressing (curative agent) for skins.

For me, in my way of life, it has always been a natural and free fuel. Wood abounds everywhere in this country of hanging coverts and big beech hedges and so in the high moorland areas do the secondary natural fuels of gorse and peat. One has only to ask a friendly farmer to let one go 'wooding' on his land, and one can get plenty.

Autumn to Spring is the time for felling and laying in these parts, so one reckons in general to get one's wood-supply in one winter as fuel for the next. I enjoy 'wooding'. It's a proper winter job and a fine vigorous occupation for a cold dry day. Off I go with my bow-saw and billhook to the place where big hedge-wood is lying or the boughs of big trees sweep low, and make a start. To limb-out lying timber you take the butt and heave it up, striking off the side-branches upwards to the top, so releasing the 'stick' from its fellows. Then you stand it up in the hedge-bank out of the way and to dry-off. This work is best done with the billhook (or hedge-chopper as it is often called) the saw being at this stage only for cutting across sticks too thick for the bill, or for taking-down live boughs. Most farmers use an axe, but I seem to get on better with a well-sharpened billhook. After a few minutes' work like this, one is glowing hot and feeling fine – with a wide view all round and the sweet fresh air in one's nostrils and muscles tingling, one is King-of-the-Castle!

When I have limbed-out enough sticks for once, I stoop to faggot-up the toppings – smaller branches – with hay-bale twine. The best of these will serve as pea-sticks and the rest, dried-out, as kindling-wood. These too are stood up against the bank.

Now there's getting the wood home. Well, on the principle of never returning empty-handed I always carry something with me on one shoulder – one big stick or two or three smaller ones. If a 'load' is properly balanced, it is surprising how great a weight can be carried on the shoulder without strain. It is the balance that matters, with this and with other things – a load should 'ride' without toppling fore or aft. Then for larger loads I have a nice little wood-trolley made for me by a kind friend, just a 'bed' and four small wheels and a towing-rope, and on this I can draw home quite a sizeable cargo. (And on this small scale one soon learns all that one needs to know about trimming a load, roping, and the dangers of load-shifting – also the difficulties of handling a vehicle without brakes or steering on slopes and curves!)

At home, the woodpile takes its stand and grows. Its natural place is as near the home-door as possible, so that it can be got-at in deep snow if that occurs. The pile must brace against a wall or bank, and each stick must stand as upright as possible, butt firmly set, weight inwards, so that the pile will neither slip nor fall. Thus set, the timber will weather-out and shed most of the rain. (Wood should never be left lying down, for thus it will draw the damp and rot.) If one has a lean-to or large shed, then some of the wood can be brought in and set to dry-out quickly ready for the first sawing.

Now when a wet day comes, one can start the sawing sessions. Under whatever cover one has one can get to work. There's no finer job on a raw winter's day for warming you up than sawing logs! As the Old Folks say, wood got this way warms you up three times: a first time when you limb it out, a second when you saw it up, and a third when you sit by its flame on the hearth! What lengths I saw it depends on what sort of fire it is for: a big hearth will take logs of a yard or more, an enclosed stove from six inches to a foot, depending on the size of the firebox. A big wood-pile, sacks of sawn logs, bags of dry kindling – one feels rich and does not fear a long hard winter.

One soon gets to know the sorts of wood with which one deals, and their properties. The wood most prevalent in these parts is beech, owing to the farm fields being enclosed by banks crested with big beech-hedges, many of which latter have reached the proportions of stands of trees. This is well, for beech is a fine wood for fuel, burning with bright flame either dry or green and equally well on hearth or stove. It is also a 'safe' wood – it does not spit in burning. Oak is to be had where there are wild woods and this burns well too, but is better dried or else used as a backstick for a slow fire. It is the hardest of woods to saw, and has a peculiar tangy scent. Ash is fairly plentiful and the finest of all woods to burn, gloriously bright either green or dry, but it is too valuable for construction-purposes to be be used for fuel other than in small left-over pieces. Withy or sallow is common, and, contrary to general opinion, burns well if thoroughly dried – but it has two drawbacks, one it is abominable to saw, jamming the saw-ribbon all the time with a peculiar sticky grip, and two, it spits in burning and is therefore unsafe. Hawthorn burns well dry, but is hard to saw and its spikes make it nasty to handle. Hazel is a poor wood to burn and Elder won't burn at all – at least I've never been able to make it. Rowan – Mountain Ash – like common Ash is too constructionally useful to burn bar odd-and-ends, and the same goes for Sycamore and Chestnut when these come to hand. Fir and Pine of various sorts one may occasionally get when any small local plantations are being thinned, and these kind all burn brilliantly, but with short life, and are all given to spitting – Larch especially is a devil and will shoot sparks right across a room. The sweet incense-like scent given-off by all the conifers is a delight however, the most pungent of all being Sitka Spruce. Elm, the worst of all woods, for burning, does not exist at all. Holly, which is prevalent in some places, burns very fiercely, dangerously so when its leaves are half-dry.

Then there's Gorse (or Furze or 'vusz' as it's known locally). Old dry gorse is one of the most inflammable things that grows and the quickest fire-starter there is. Once upon a time it was faggoted for bread-ovens and even pottery-kilns. I myself am probably the last person to faggot gorse in these parts. This I used to do when I lived in an ancient cottage with a big open hearth. It is a job that needs a strong staff-hook and a pair of leather (hedger's) gloves. Once set alight on a hearth such a faggot burns with a sheet of flame and intensity of heat as is unequalled by any other fuel – I would have backed my iron kettle hanging on the back-crook above the blaze against an electric kettle in boiling-time. But gorse consumes itself with its own fierce heat very quickly, and needs to be backed by more substantial fuel for a lasting fire.

Lastly, there is Peat. In former times peat, which is the stuff of the black bogs of this moorland country, was dug extensively by all the hill-country householders for their hearth fires. I have dug and used some from time to time, and it makes a slow steady incense-sweet fire, the ashes of which remain hot and live all night. For brightness though, one needs some cheerful wood with it, for of itself it has little flame.

So back to the home-fire again. Having established a fuel supply the efficiency and comfort of a wood fire depends on the knowledge and management of it. First of all necessary things (that is, next after the means of striking fire itself, which in my case is the commonplace of matches) is a steady supply of dry kindling-wood. Always one must ensure this: small gorse-faggots or sacks of dry twigs and small-broken sticks must be stored in a dry place, and every time one has a fire, one should crisp-out by its warmth enough quick-kindling for the *next* fire. Another thing, any stick more than a half-inch round should be split – young flames will catch more readily on sharp edges than on the round. Thus the new fire will go away at a touch with no messing-about.

No two fireplaces, whether hearth or stove, will burn alike. Each is an individual and must be understood. For some the logs must be laid long ways, for others end-outwards or tentwise. You have to learn the ways and likes of your particular fire – if you don't it will sulk and smoke! Once understood, though, your fire is friend and lifegiver, and as handy to cook and heat as any modern sophisticated appliance.

So to light a fire again, the oldest act of home-making: kneel before its layings in cold and darkness, perhaps with aching wet fingers and soaking clothes, strike the light, see the small flame take hold, then the flare, the crackle, the blaze of triumph! – glorious light, heat, a singing kettle and all comforts for the night! Life, hearth and home! And on my knees I give thanks.

CHAPTER FIVE

Harvest of the Wild

NATURE is the giver of all, and her bounty is great. All around me lies the land, moor and field, marsh and wood, and here as the seasons come and go I may find a harvest of many things. Food to eat, wood for my fire, flowers for my home, beauty to delight my senses, inspiration for my work.

The roots of life are deep in the earth, but so many folk nowadays, receiving the necessities of life in the form of packaged and manufactured goods see not this and seem blind to its fact. Insulated from the facts of life, they know not, or seem not to know, anything of earth and climate and what these together bring forth. Here in my way of life I see it first hand, heaven and earth together giving water, food, fuel, materials for building, space and beauty for nourishment of the soul as well as the body, and I profit thereby.

For me Nature gives sustenance two-fold: a patch of earth on which I can cultivate by my own labour the nourishing vegetables that are my staff of life, and the benison of all those offerings of her own which in due season I may have for the taking without cost or effort.

The first of all blessings is the sweet water that I drink from the spring in the hill, or from the stream below when the first runs dry. Oh, how precious it is, sparkling and life-giving, running bright and clear from its source under rushes and bog-plants. How I give thanks for it as I dip my jug into its crystal rill, uncontaminated by horrid chemicals, and therefrom fill my bucket. (Well, yes, after a heavy spate of rain it is apt to be coffee-coloured – but that's only once in a while.)

Then in their season come all the herbs and fruits of the wild earth. As I write it is mid-February, and soon I shall be looking for the first green shoots of the nettles that abound around the old farm as they do about every country homestead. As soon as I espy these out I go with basket and a pair of scissors and nip and flip them in (being very careful not to touch or be touched by them, for it is in the Spring that their sting is most virulent) and convey them to the cooking-pot. Boiled lightly with other vegetables, or in a stew, they are very palatable, having a nutty flavour, and extremely nourishing. (The sting goes out of them in the first moments of boiling.) Once-upon-a-time, in the days before patent medicines, boiled nettles were well-known as a Spring tonic, being the first green-leaved things to appear after the winter, and full of minerals, etc. After all, consider, why has the nettle found it necessary to arm itself with such a vicious sting in all its parts at all stages of growth? The answer is simple: because it is so tasty and nourishing it would be eaten out of existence by grazing animals were it not so armed – and the same goes for other spiked things such as thistles, gorse and holly.

The next herb to be looked for – usually one has not far to seek in this country – is the sorrel. This small relative of the dock early puts forth its unmistakable barbed-spear or arrow shaped leaves in the hedge-banks and old meadows, and these leaves picked and eaten raw are one of the most delicious of salad herbs, having a distinctive sharp savoury taste. (They can also be used in stews, but to me it always seems a shame to cook such lovely fresh leaves.) Incidentally, sorrel leaves should be picked only a few minutes before they are to be eaten, as they wither very quickly.

Then as Spring advances the cresses flourish. Best of them all is the watercress, but this is not always as plentiful as one would wish in moorland country, partly because it much prefers pools of still water to rushing streams, partly because in this stock-raising region it is much relished and eaten by grazing animals. But any wild cress is tasty, and every where in odd corners – especially on bits of fallow garden – I can find the little penny-cress as a tasty morsel. Such a dainty little thing it is, that it really seems a shame to eat it!

By the stream there is peppermint, and under the hedges the shamrock-leaved wood-sorrel. Lamb's-lettuce springs in waste places and many another green thing which is edible if you have a taste for it. But it is the season of fruit to which I look forward most.

First of the summer's fruits are the wild strawberries. Exquisite things in colour and flavour, scarlet pendants under the hedges and along the crannied walls. (If fairies have food, then wild strawberries must be their feast!) Their flavour is the very quintessence of their kind, unmatched by any garden strain, and every tiny fruit is a delight to the tongue.

Next come the whortleberries – worts as they are commonly called. These are children of the moor, growing only about or above the 1,000 ft. contour, their low bushes intermingling with the heather and dwarf gorse or tufting the lonely stone walls that run out across the lonely hills and heaths. They come with the first heather-bloom of July and August, and many a pleasant hour I recall picking the sun-warmed blue-black berries from the rim of a bank whilst the bees hum in the heather-bells (devils they are to pick though, slipping through your fingers all the while). Myself, I eat them all raw – I never cook them, despite the fact that whortleberry tart or pie is an Exmoor tradition, for to my taste they are insipid when cooked, loosing all their natural piquant flavour thuswise.

By late July and onwards to September one may look for the wild raspberries. In this region the wild raspberry is often as plentiful, or more so, than the bramble, growing in thickets amongst the bracken on steep hillsides and along the hedge-banks of field and lane. Its canes drip with dusky crimson fruits in due season, and of all the wild berries it is, next after the wild strawberry, the most exquisitely flavoured. A raspberry expedition makes a walk worth while!

Elder-trees offer heady bunches of coal-black berries now. Many things one can make with elder fruit from jams to wine, but I prefer them raw, though their peculiar flavour is not to every-one's taste. Dark sloes too deck the blackthorn, but I find them acid to the point of bitterness, so mostly leave them alone. Gloriously scarlet the rowan-berries blaze on the mountain-ash, but so far I have not been tempted to eat them, though I know they are full of vitamins – chiefly I think because they are so splendid against the sky that it seems sacrilege to touch them. Likewise the rose-hips on the hedge-briers are so decorative that I hate to disturb them.

Last of the season come the blackberries. A noble thing is a fine blackberry, big, juicy and jet-black, luscious to eat. Never does one need to look far, for the arching stems with spreading ornate leaves (and ferocious hooked prickles) of the bramble are everywhere, or almost everywhere, along the hedge-banks, about old buildings, and making mats on moory hillsides. In a good year the berries hang in dark and glossy profusion, autumn food for man and bird, but they are seldom fully ripe before mid-September, and will carry their crop through October and even into November, until the frosts put an end to it.

Delicious sun-ripened blackberries! They come to close the fruiting year with their richness, shining jet amongst the reds and golds of autumn leaves. What handfuls I eat as I walk lanes and field-ways! What a feast they offer! What memories too I have of many black-berryings with jug in hand for taking home, and hands stained with purple juice and lips likewise from the eating! Again I say, all my fruit I eat raw – such delicious delicacies of the wild it seems sin to cook – why do so many people seem driven by an inexplicable mania to *cook* everything?

Ere the blackberries are spent the mushrooms come. Buttons of dusky white pink-lipped amongst the meadow-grass or heather. Bigger bolder ones tawny and brown-gilled in other places, mysterious treasure born of the dark earth and the morning dew, touched by the September sun. What pleasure there is in mushrooming! The espying of the precious offerings from afar, the touching of them with my finger-tips as I pick them – that curious exquisite velvety feel – the fragrant earthy smell, then the blissful nibble! As with the fruit, I eat my mushrooms raw, just as they are, delighting in the fresh indefinable flavour. Why do most folk positively *murder* delicious mushrooms by first peeling them and then frying or boiling them?

Other fungi there are too, for this wild wet land brings forth strange children in the autumn days, pallid or lurid as the case may be, but I do not eat any of them. Some I know *are* edible, but, equally, some are highly poisonous, so I leave them be, taking no risk of mistaken identity.

Last on the list come nuts. Hereabouts hazel bushes abound and in a good year hazel-nuts are plentiful. But they must be gathered at just the right time in October, for take them too early and the kernels will not have filled out, leave them too late and the squirrels and other small beasties will have them. Of what I can get, I eat some right away – for fresh, they are crisp and delicious in a way kept nuts never are – and some I store away for Christmas.

Since beech is prevalent everywhere, beech-nuts are shed in masses by the bigger trees every year. Small, and like the worts tedious to pick, nevertheless they are fine little nuts, and most years I pick up a bagful for the winter. Other nuts are rarely come by. Walnuts do not grow at this altitude and Chestnuts – I have some 'Spanish' trees here in the windbreak – do not set edible nuts.

Sometimes passing through oak-woods I pick up acorns to nibble, and find them very nice, but I am careful not to eat too many at once, since I have heard they contain some toxic element.

The climax of Nature's offering, beyond the gift of plants, is wild meat, but of this I have written much elsewhere, so will not encumber this little chapter with such detail.

Food to eat is but one of the harvests of the wild. Flowers for delight of colour and scent, and lovely foliage, are also the gift of Nature. All the year round I may gather a bunch of beautiful things, so that even if I had not a flower-garden of my own, I might have always a vase of flowers to cheer my little home. Snowdrops from a copse in February and pendant hazel-catkins to go with them, then primroses from the sunny banks, and after them bluebells, red campions, fronds of ferns, buttercups, spiring fox gloves and all the host of summer flowers and tall shining grasses. Then the glory of purple heather to round the autumn (Sweet peas mingled with heather in a copper kettle: this is one of my favourite arrangements). Even when the flowers are gone, there are bright berries still and late red and gold leaves, and even in the depths of winter glossy ivy-leaves and graceful twigs. And at Christmas fir and holly, as much as I want! I pluck sparingly of all these treasures, though, for they are to be loved and cherished, not ravished.

Other things too, the wide moor offers: rushes for stuffing mattresses (there is no more comfortable bed than one of springy rush) or for thatching if one should wish to essay this. Fern (bracken) for bedding any beast one has, or for adding to the compost heap – bracken makes fine compost.

Then there's peat for fuel, and gorse and wood – about which I have already written.

Deepest of all, Nature offers its own sheer wonder to the dweller within its world. The majesty of landscape under the cloud-sailing sky. The marvel of leaf and flower and every living thing. The inspiration to create with pencil and brush some personal, perhaps immortal, thing from the transient moment.

This too is a harvest from the hand of Nature.

H.L.B.

CHAPTER SIX

The Gift of a Garden

Rows of fresh green vegetables in the summer sun, glossy cabbages, tall peas, and beans, scarlet runners reaching for the sky, onions drying on the warm earth, tousle-headed potatoes and lines of all sorts of other things. Strawberry-beds under the high top bank; a herb-patch by the gate giving off scents of mint, marjoram, thyme, sage, peppermint and lemon-balm; Sweet peas gay along the bottom fence. Tubs of brilliant dahlias, marigolds, nasturtiums, pansies and Cape-daisies ranged in a flowering mass along the front of the barn. Borders of hardy plants about a small lawn with a sundial in the midst. This is my garden, my staff of life which gives me food to eat and the joy of flowers for delight.

For me, the most precious thing in the world, next after a home itself, is a garden. All my life I've been a gardener, ever since as a small child I had my own little plot. Without a garden I could hardly live. A garden is both a pleasure and a very practical thing, a patch on which you grow your own food and from which I, at least, sustain myself in independence and health. The produce of a garden will keep you and nourish you when all else fails. Fresh vegetables, fruit and herbs will not only feed you in terms of filling your stomach, they will give you better health than all the packaged and processed foods in the world, and all the doctor's medicines too.

Let no one imagine though, that gardening, especially gardening in a hill-country, is an easy simple thing. It calls for much hard work (at least in the initial stages of garden-making) a knowledge of plants and their ways of growth, and a deep understanding of the nature of the land itself. Nor let it be thought that gardening is a sweet and innocent thing. It is not. One must be forever fighting and killing, slaughtering both weeds and wild life, in order to protect and maintain your little kingdom of soil within a hard land and under a difficult climate.

A true hill-country garden is a garden in the wilderness, fashioned with loving care in the midst of a harsh land and in the teeth of hostile elements, an intensely personal patch from which one looks out upon moor and heath as from a fastness upon unconquered territory, and holds with the strength of one's hand against invading forces.

No gentleness is there in gardening here. Like a pioneer, one must break one's ground in enemy territory. Like a garrison commander one must hold the fort against ever-pressing foes. One must erect barriers against the rapacity of sheep, cattle and ponies, and patrol these fences with regularity. One must have a gun at the ready in the evening hours against invading rabbits, hares and sometimes deer, and in the early mornings against woodpigeons. One must practise the ancient skill of the trapper in the war against mice, voles and moles. One must become a very Borgia in the art of poisoning slugs, bugs and other pests.

One must also do battle against all the hordes and legions of wild weeds ever marching down the hills to repossess one's small precious patch. One must spend more hours erecting screens for beloved plants against tempestuous winds, and coverings against late frost, than ever one will have to sit in one's Paradise. It is war from first to last.

I have made many gardens, having had many homes, and all of them I have had either to reclaim from dereliction or break from the wilderness-ground. So, all that I know about hill-country gardening has been learnt the hard way.

Having dealt with the essential fencing and clearance (as in a previous chapter) gardening proper may be said to consist of five parts: an understanding of the local soil and climate; the layout of a garden, making best use of available terrain; soil fertility, its creation and maintenance; the practical growing of plants, both vegetables for food and flowers for delight; and the art of creating visual pleasure, i.e. landscaping and adding ornamental features.

The understanding of regional conditions – that is, soil and underlying geology, climate, particular position and altitude – are vital, especially in a tough hill-country like this. (Lack of this appreciation has been the downfall of many newcomers, both gardeners and farmers, in these parts.) You cannot garden, any more than you can farm, here on the high moor as you do in the low country.

Of this, my beloved Exmoor, it may be said that the high altitude (most of the land being above 1,000 ft.) and proximity to the Atlantic Ocean give a climate that is very wet, whilst the underlying ancient sandstones, grits and shales make a soil which is mostly thin and very acid. The wild wind that sweeps in from the sea is an enemy to be reckoned with, and the long wet winters make Spring very late. April is a winter month, and May often little better, bringing with it bitter late frosts that do cruel damage to early plants. On the other hand, though, heavy dews keep the land refreshed in summer, the autumns are mild and long-drawn-out, and winter proper does not set in until after Christmas. On the whole, the climate being an Atlantic one, snow-fall is not generally heavy – excepting in a phenominal winter like '63. So, it is to these conditions one must adapt one's gardening.

Something else too, it is good to observe: the nature of the local flora. By taking note of what grows wild, one may get a fair idea of what sort of plants will flourish in a garden and what will not. Looking all around I see heather, the inevitable bracken and gorse, ferns of all sorts, primroses, bluebells and all the acid-tolerant flowers and shrubs of moor, meadow, bog and wood. Whortleberries, wild strawberries, wild raspberries and brambles abound, also sloes and hazel-nuts, but no crabapples. Thus, in gardening, I have found the cultivated relatives of these plants do well, whilst those others not in harmony with the nature of the land have to be coaxed and some, such as apples, will not do at all.

The first requisite of a good garden is a sunny position. No garden, particularly a vegetable garden, will do well if it does not enjoy full sun. This is to say, it must have a southerly aspect. Yet it must be sheltered, with windbreaks not only on the north side but south-west and east as well. One must make a careful balance between the need for sunshine and air and the need for shelter. Of the winds that blow so fiercely across this country, the greatest come from S.W. to N.W. (true ocean storms, these) and the coldest, the snowladen blizzards and icy winds of late winter, from N. and N.E.

If a garden can be sited on a southerly slope, so much the better, for thus it will lie in the sun and be well-drained (a consideration in this wet climate) also the frost will tend to roll away downwards from it.

Soil is the most vital of things for the gardener. Upon its fertility depends all that grows, which in the case of the self-supporting person like myself is almost life itself. If its fertility fails, so do the crops of the gardener and farmer, and hunger stalks man and beast. Now I myself am an organic gardener, believing that fertility and health is best maintained by the principle of whatever comes from the soil should be returned to the soil. So the basis of my gardening is the compost-heap. A large heap, five feet wide and as long and high as need be takes first place in my vegetable garden. Into it goes every scrap of organic matter, animal and vegetable, I can lay my hands on. All weeds, vegetable residues, hedge and lawn-trimmings, cut bracken and old hay, such cattle and sheep droppings as lie near to hand, fur, feathers and guts from sporting occasions, and, last but not least, the nightly contents of an earth-closet. So the heap, inter-layed with earth spread like a sandwich-filling, mounts up all through the year and by February is ready to be dug into the garden-plots when a break of dry weather occurs. This is my only manure, and the wood-ash (collected from my home-fire) with which I dress growing plants in the Spring my only fertilizer. I use neither 'artificials' nor lime. I go on the principle that if everything goes into the soil via the compost-heap, then everything is there – all minerals, etc. – and the plants will find what they want. Also, a soil kept rich in the resulting humus remains moist in dry weather and fairly well-drained in wet, so providing plants with good living conditions. Beyond this, I practise a rotation of crops on as long a course as I can according to the size of the garden (in order to have an adequate supply of some basic vegetables it is sometimes necessary to have larger plots than fit a long rotation) and consider five years about right. Also, I try to 'subsoil' a part of the garden each year: this is not the same thing as deep-digging, but the breaking of the subsoil with a fork without bringing it to the top. This both drains and airs the ground.

Next comes the understanding of plants, how they grow, what they like and desire in general, and what individual sorts like or loathe in particular. All plants need an adequate amount of air, space, sunshine, water and fertile mineral-laden soil, also shelter from the harsher extremes of climate and protection from predatory animals. There however generalization ends, for different plants have different desires. Some demand very rich soil, some do best on moderate soil. Some like an acid soil and can't abide lime, others have a fondness for lime. (Though, with regards the latter, I have found that those which *don't* like lime vastly outnumbered those which do, and the few that *do* seem able

31

to get along reasonably well without it provided their other needs are met with – hence my refraining from indiscriminate lime-spreading.) Some like full strong sun, others like partial shade. Some like a lot of moisture, others prefer comparatively dry conditions. It is the art of the gardener to find out which likes what, for upon this, success in raising plants depends.

Under the heading of 'growing things' must come pest-control, for if you do not control pests you will assuredly grow nothing at all. The larger pests having been considered in the context of fencing, the lesser ones can be enumerated as birds, moles, voles, mice, slugs, snails and bugs. Against each adequate measures must be taken. For birds the best thing is netting, for voles and mice trapping (just ordinary mousetraps baited with a little brown bread or raw potato, but they must be covered with something to prevent birds getting caught) for snails, etc. slug-bait under stones (or the revolting practice of 'slugging' ie. going round the garden after dark with a torch and a pair of scissors, nipping each crawling gastropod into two halves), for bugs of various sorts derris or pyrethrum (I do not use sprays nor strong pesticides, only the relatively mild derris). This only leaves moles and I confess I have no foolproof remedy against moles. Moles are a prime pest in as much as they are so difficult to deal with. One can try anything from traps to mothballs – sometimes these work and sometimes they don't.

Concerning disease, I get so little that I don't do anything about it, except to remove the few affected bits of leaf if or when it occurs.

As a practical gardener, gardening to live, my main preoccupation has to be with vegetables, i.e. food-production. I have to grow for myself a balance of potatoes, root-vegetables (carrots and parsnips), onions, shallots and leeks, greenstuff (cabbages, kale, broccoli, etc.), peas and beans, celery, marrows, rhubarb and herbs of all sorts. Also such luxuries as cucumbers and tomatoes and strawberries. The only things I don't bother to grow are swedes and turnips, as these are a field-crop on the hill-farms, grown for feeding-off to sheep in the winter, and it is more expedient to scrounge from a friend's field than to have to devote a portion of an already overcrowded garden to these space-demanding things.

My present vegetable garden is a small one, no more I think than four square rods (the West Country rod or pole being a length of $5\frac{1}{2}$ yards, a square rod is an area of $30\frac{1}{4}$ square yards). Into this has to go all the aforesaid, on a system of tight rotation and catch-cropping. On the whole I think it is fair to say this small patch of earth produces for me a yearly average of some seven hundredweight of good fresh food. This is arrived at by the following averages: potatoes 3 cwt., roots 2 cwt., onions, etc. 1 cwt., green vegetables 1 cwt. This in turn averages out at about 2 lb. of good food per day. (Some folk have doubted this, saying it would barely be possible to get 3 cwt. of potatoes of the whole of the area, but in simple terms this is arrived at by planting a quarter of the garden (one square rod) with 112 roots of spuds approximately one foot apart in rows about 2' 6" apart, and then persuading them to crop at an average of 3 lb. a root = 3 cwt. Of course it takes some hard work with heavy composting and deep ridging to get a constantly good crop, some years being naturally better or worse, but on the whole it works out thus.)

As to the health and vigour of my vegetables, and spuds in particular, I constantly save my seed of peas, broad and runner beans (and some other things in a good year) and my own potato tubers. The best of my spud strains I have had and kept going for about twenty years now. There has been no deterioration, rather the reverse, for stuff seems to thrive from being acclimatised.

Flowers for pleasure are the joy of life, the crown of a garden, the delight of a gardener. No matter how full a plot must needs be with prosaic vegetables, I always find room for a few flowers. More than a few if I can, filling all odd corners and even old buckets with the dear gay things. Snowdrops, daffodils and narcissus, primroses, polyanthus, forget-me-nots and pansies for the Spring, sweet-williams and shrub-roses – plus some other hardy herbacious plants – for early summer, a show of many gay annuals in tubs of all sorts for high summer and autumn, with a few more late perennial plants. (Needless to say, those plants do best which like an acid soil, and I am always intending to establish heaths and heathers and rhododendrons, but the latter are expensive to buy.)

How I fuss over them, with what eagerness I go out on sunny mornings to see what seedlings have come up, what buds have opened! Gardening is a vocation, a dedication, for the gardener goes hand-in-hand with life, living with the days and the waxing and waning of the seasons. He that has a garden can never be lonely nor empty-hearted nor divorced from life.

A garden binds a house to its site and one's own self to a plot of earth. Put flowers around a dwelling, bring a few in and put in a vase, and the place is Home. As one progresses with garden-making, the garden ceases to be a wholly utjlitarian thing and becomes something expressive of the land and earth from which it is sprung and of one's own personality and response. Now it becomes a true art, an art-form composing itself of earth and sun and living forms and colours and textures, of water, of distance and pure space. One sets grass against rock, smooth stone against heady plants, shape against shape, colour against colour, texture against texture, creates vistas, frames distant views, sets an ornament to guide the eye. One channels water to reflect the sky or sing under branches, or plants a tree to cast a shadow across a sunlit lawn. Unconsciously, one fashions things to express emotions and perceptions for which there are no words. One has entered into the realms of living poetry.

In my tough life I have, alas, little time or scope for such things, but I have left small trees for dappled shadow, made a simple sundial for a focal-point, set paving-stones across a patch of lawn and a square of white trellis to uphold a honeysuckle, and these small things give me added pleasure.

So in the end, despite its element of ruthlessness, a garden is a thing of joy, affording sustenance to the body and delight to the senses, and for me my .fragment of earthly paradise.

CHAPTER SEVEN

Hunter's World

THE crack of a rifle-shot echoes down the valley ... again I hold my rifle in my hands and walk the evening rounds.

It is my most precious and proudest possession, this Marlin rifle, my wilderness companion, giver of meat, slayer of vermin, defender if needbe. Without it my life would be incomplete, less satisfying, more difficult. It goes with me on arm or back as I go the rounds of my territory, and at night it lies on the hangers above my head ready to hand if needed.

To me it is a thing of beauty, a delight to handle. A thing of perfect precision, perfect craftsmanship, a superb combination of blue steel and polished walnut, of deadly power and perfect form. As I bring it up to shoot, it slides into my hands with a grace that makes it an extension of myself, and as I carry it, its very weight is company to me.

A gun is indeed the proudest possession anyone can have. The modern successor to the bow and the javelin, the missile weapon supreme, it is one of the things that has exalted man above the rest of animal life. With it you have the power to get meat to eat and to protect your territory against predators. It also proclaims personal pride and freedom – the right of the free man to 'keep and bear arms'.

Together with the rifle goes my ammunition-belt, very handsome with its shining brass shells (I call it my Mexican belt!) and upon another belt my hunting-knife. Thus equipped, the hunter's world of wild wood, hill and valley is mine.

Now, of guns and their sorts and uses, there is so much to say that I had best not say it at all, lest this chapter be as long as the rest of the book, but I will enlarge a little on knives. Everyone who lives with Nature should possess a powerful knife.

The choice of a knife is a personal matter, but my preference is always for a sheath-knife. My reasons are, firstly, a sheath-knife is always there on your hip to be reached for at a moment's notice with one hand only. One does not need to use two hands to have it at the ready, and this is important, as in the circumstances in which you need it you usually have something grasped in the other hand. With a clasp-knife you have to use two hands to open the blade for use, and so are forced to relinquish your hold on whatever else you are hanging on to. Secondly, it is a safer sort of knife to have and handle. There is no chance, as by a hasty twist in an unguarded moment, of having the blade close on your fingers, such as there is with a clasp-knife. (I had this latter happen to me once, long ago – luckily the knife was not a very powerful one, so I've still got my fingers!)

A hunting-knife should be as strong as possible, heavy in the hand but not over-long in the blade. The best sort is one with blade about five inches long, back almost a quarter-inch thick and ridged for thumb-hold when skinning, point a cutaway curve and under-edge sharp as a razor. (A long blade of six or seven inches, though impressive, is apt to be awkward in practical use, especially for skinning, where a short blade is handiest.) Incidentally, a knife of such a pattern is also known as a Bowie-knife.

What, say certain friends, 'do you *do* with a carcass when you've got it? Well, as Mrs Beaton is said to have said, 'first catch your hare, then cook it'. So I will begin at the beginning, which is with killing.

In order to kill cleanly and efficiently, it is necessary to know how to kill. This entails a basic knowledge of anatomy and the vital areas. The cleanest and most merciful shot is the brain or head-shot. Just one bullet in the centre of the brain and the beast goes down without knowing what has hit it, and that is the end. The head-shot however, is only to be taken at close range and by a reasonably skilled marksman, for the chance of hitting the jaws instead of the head proper and so letting a cruelly wounded beast go off to die in misery, is too great.

The heart is the next most certain killing-place, but like the brain it is a very small area, and since it lies low in an animal's forehand the risk of breaking a leg and so letting a crippled animal escape is likewise great. A neck-shot is good, but again the target small. Generally speaking, at all fairly long ranges the best shot is the shoulder, or lung-shot. (Yes, I know you spoil a bit of meat this way, but it is *sure*.) If you aim to put your bullet into the hollow of the shoulder, that is, just behind the point, then you are bound to hit something vital as this is the middle of the 'power house'. Incidentally, the proper weapon for such shooting, is rabbit or hare .22, anything larger .240 or heavier.

Having killed your beast, if you wish the meat to keep well (assuming it is a large beast) you should cut its throat to let the blood out. Here is the first office for the hunting-knife.

So, assuming the beast has been got home by some means or other, the first step is to gut it to lessen the weight (being careful in so doing to set aside the liver, kidneys and heart on a dish, for these are most tasty morsels). Then take off the head and get this out of the way. Then thrust a stout stake through the hamstrings behind the hocks, fasten a rope to the middle, throw over a beam, and heave until your carcass is suspended at a convenient height. (Just how heavy dead-weight is, you will soon find! However, by this time you will probably have found a friend to help you.)

To skin, continue the belly-split from vent to throat, make four radial cuts from this out along the inner sides of the limbs, then circular cuts around the legs where you wish the hide to terminate. Now starting peeling the skin off downwards, using the knife with a short flicking motion. (And be careful of your fingers – a skinning-knife sharp enough to do its work properly is sharp enough to cut your fingers off!) As soon as the skin is off, should you wish to keep it for curing, you must spread salt or wood-ash on the raw side to prevent deterioration.

Finally, dismembering the carcass – with hack-saw split the spine right down clean, then take off quarters and shoulders with knife. Further sub-divide or joint-up meat as preferred. And now you've turned meat-on-the-hoof into meat-for-the-table!

The above is the proper, or at least the simplest way of dealing with any carcass above the size of a rabbit.

Now to deal with the hide. There are in fact many methods of curing skins, but for me the simplest and most satisfactory way is that of dry-curing with salt and alum, soda, or wood ash. I go about it this way – take the raw skin – which will already have been salted as soon as it was off the carcass – and throw it hair downwards on the ground, spreading it out wide. Take four sticks or poles and lay four-square about the skin and tie cross-ended so that you have a frame a little larger than the spread skin. Then stretch out the hide and nail or lace with strong string to the frame, straining it taut in a good shape. You can now turn the whole thing over or stand it up, and at this stage wash off any mud, blood or muck from the hair. Having done this, get to work with a blunt knife (with a sharp one at this stage you run too much risk of puncturing the skin) and flay of all shreds of fat or meat still adhering to the skin until it is just skin and nothing more. Then take alum, or if you have not this to hand, soda (bicarbonate will do) or wood ash and rub this (dry) evenly into the raw side. Then stand up in an airy shed to dry-off, or when fine put out in the sun to assist this. Round-about three weeks is the average time the treated hide will take to cure-out, gradually drying-off and turning to a leathery-parchment texture. You then cut your skin off the frame, and there's a fine new rug!

This method is suitable for all sorts and sizes of skins, remembering only that different amounts of curing-agents are needed according to size. Roughly, of alum, eight ounces for deer or calf, four for sheep, less for fox or hare, less still for rabbit, grey squirrel or mink. Of soda, somewhat more, because it is less strong; of wood-ash, as much as you can lard onto the skin (incidentally, skins can be cured-out with wood-ash only, without the use of salt, providing you do it at once, immediately after skinning). Skins so cured will not deteriorate, but since they are not tanned, they will always tend to stiffen in hot dry weather and then go limp again in a damp atmosphere. Oh, and one thing I have not mentioned: that before I lace the skin on the frame I usually pour paraffin over the hair-side – this is partly to serve as an insecticide (most animals have 'lodgers' and it is best to get rid of them at this stage) and partly because paraffin itself is something of a preservative.

Coming to ethics – sometimes I am asked, do I not feel for the creatures that I kill, and loving all Nature how can I bear to do so? The answer is, simply, that in living with Nature one perceives that death is a part of life, and killing part of Nature's law and pattern. Living with Nature is very different from looking at it in pictures. Nature in her wonderful web of life is both infinitely beautiful and infinitely cruel. All creatures kill to live in some way or another. Even lambs eat grass, which is a very beautiful form of life. Foxes kill lambs. Crows pick the eyes and tongue out of a living sheep when it is down and helpless. The wood-pigeons would decimate my garden if I did not stop them. Nature is utterly ruthless in all her ways. The trouble with being sentimental about Nature is that Nature is not sentimental about you. There is a point beyond which you must not let yourself be sentimental about Nature, else you will not survive yourself.

Then for me personally there is the fact that I am a heavy meat-eater – at least when I get the chance. Some folk seem able to be vegetarians and thrive, but I cannot. When I do not have meat in my diet I miss it terribly and do not have quite the same vigour. So I kill to eat, as do all other creatures, directly or indirectly, for meat, and to protect my garden-produce which is so vital to me. I do not think it is possible to live face to face with Nature without killing. So I live in a hunter's world, pitting myself against the wiles of the wild things.

Then there's the urge to hunt. Hunting is a natural instinct, one of the deepest and most fundamental there is. Long, long ago at the dawn of life Man was a hunter before he was anything else, and society itself arose on the ways of the hunting band. The urge to hunt is in every man.

As to the impact of man on Nature through hunting, this, within the safeguards of close seasons and a humane code, is wholly beneficial. All animals must be controlled in their numbers – in a state of truly wild Nature this would be done by the grand predators such as lions, panthers and wolves, but where these have been exterminated by Man for his own ends, then Man himself must take their place. Field-sports, properly practised, are both a means of control and a means of preservation of a species, and link agriculture and conservation hand-in-hand.

Hunting too is a communion with Nature. Whether hunting with horse and hound or stalking game with a gun, you become a part of wild Nature, entering into a world of elemental instincts and animal senses. You must be as alert and as enduring as the beasts you hunt. Consider, every animal in its own sphere and on its own territory is superior to Man: who can run like a deer, jink like a hare, see like a crow, scent like a fox, hear like a rabbit? To match them, you must learn their ways and be more cunning and physically tougher than they. From this comes sharpness of the senses and great bodily vigour and fitness. He that hunts is alive, aware of being, and enjoying better health than the man who does not.

So to hunt! So many memories I have, and hopes of days to come. Of the sound of a huntsman's horn on a grey winter morning, the red of his coat like a splash of blood under the dripping trees, the cry of the hounds as they sweep down the dark hillside like a flight of seabirds, the distant drumming of hooves setting my heart pounding to their rhythm. Or an icy December dawn, crouched with a companion amongst the frosted bushes betwixt the root-field and the dark oak-wood, the red glow of sunrise glinting on rifle barrels, waiting, waiting ... The sunset light of an autumn evening, and creeping, stalking down the hedges and round the gateways, every sense alert, for just a rabbit to fill the pot ... He has not lived who has not hunted!

CHAPTER EIGHT

Daily Bread and Other Food

BREAD is said to be the Staff of Life, that food which has sustained civilized Man through all the ages since he first discovered the wonderful grain called wheat, and for which we are bidden to ask and to be thankful.

Now there is nothing nicer than good crusty nutty wholemeal bread, but I myself eat very little of it because my diet, like my economics, is somewhat different to other peoples. The corner-stone of my economy and independence being self-sufficiency, I produce most of my food for myself, which is to say, vegetables and meat, and so in fact buy very little of anything. It is my own little garden which is my staff of life.

Of gardening proper I have said much elsewhere, stressing the fact that I am an organic gardener, growing all my vegetables on home-made compost, so I will here simply appraise my garden produce in terms of food. Enough to say, I have developed some very strong convictions over the years concerning the relationship between soil, food and health – but there, I will probably say a bit more before I've finished this chapter.

What do I grow to be self-sufficient? Firstly, potatoes. Good honest spuds are the filler-up of a hungry tummy and take the place of bread as a bulkfood. You've always got a meal if you've got a potato in the house – boil it, bake it, fry it, slice it, mash it, eat it whole or make it into a little cake, it will fill, nourish and sustain you. It's something you can have all the year round too, because it's storable from one season to the next. For myself I need at least 1 lb a day, twice that if I can get it, so must grow a minimum of 3 cwt. on my little garden, which of course I do, and since the garden is so small try to get a patch somewhere 'lying out' for extra. Potatoes as such are of immense variety, early or maincrop, firm or floury, epicurean or heavy-cropping, but if I had to choose just one sort, I think I would settle for the old Majestic, for it combines in itself all good qualities – it has good flavour, can be dug as an 'early', is a very heavy cropper, resistant to disease, and a sound keeper.

Next comes the 'root' group of vegetables: swedes, turnips, carrots, parsnips, etc., which also provide bulk and are available all through the winter for the making of delicious stews. Of the first two I prefer swedes, as they have a finer flavour, and of swedes themselves I like the good old field 'cow swede' with its strong taste and deep orange-gold colour.

Onions, shallots and leeks are a 'must' for no stew is complete without one or the other. The first two are to be stored for the winter, the last I leave on the ground to pull as I want, for they are not only at their best with white stems in early Spring, but their leaves provide a green vegetable at a time when other stuff may be scarce.

Then greenstuff, which term embraces a variety of things. First, the all-important brassica group. All-important I say, because I believe for good health one should eat fresh green-leaf vegetables every day, and I say every day, for with proper garden management one should be able to go into the garden 365 days a year and come out with some sort of 'greens'. If a proper succession of Spring cabbages, summer cabbages, broccoli, winter Savoys, Brussels sprouts and Kale is arranged, then one *can* do so. If really hardy varieties of the winter sorts are grown, then the hardest weather will not kill them and you can go out in January and kick the snow and ice off them and still take in good fresh stuff.

Then there are peas and beans. Peas and runner-beans count as green summer vegetables, but broad-beans are in a class on their own, being a curiously filling almost 'meaty' vegetable. If I had enough ground I would grow enough of them to dry for the winter.

Of herbs proper and salad vegetables I grow a variety (as well as culling wild sorts from Nature) for not only are they health-giving – their medicinal value made them the first cultivated plants in the gardens of our ancestors – but their piquant flavours add zest to the plainest dishes.

Fruit I love, and eat as much of it as I can, when I can, and I grow some very fine strawberries along one side of my garden, but most of it Nature provides from moor and hedge row, to the extent that I may eat fresh fruit from Midsummer to the end of October. Rhubarb (of which I have large clumps) I rank as a fruit, and it fills a gap from early Spring – by which time any apples I may have been given are finished – until strawberry-time.

Also, most years I manage to provide myself with such luxuries as cucumbers and tomatoes, grown out-doors under a sunny wall.

So much for the vegetable kingdom, which supplies me with my basic food. Next meat.

Now some people seem to be able to exist as vegetarians. I cannot. By nature I am a heavy meat-eater, and find a big hole in my life and diet when I do not get plenty of meat. My idea of a fair ration of meat is a pound a day, to be eaten for breakfast. Sometimes I get it, sometimes I don't. Needless to say, butcher's meat is expensive and I can't afford to buy it. So how do I manage? Well, just as my garden grows vegetables, so this country grows meat, and I get my fair share of it.

Of the shooting and preparing of meat, I have already said a good deal, so what I now say is specifically about meat as a food. Meat – according to my experience – contains concentrated energy-power unequalled by anything else. Theoretically, a handful of raisins, nuts, or beans (and I *am* fond of all three) may contain the equivalent amount of whatever-it-is that gives strength, but in *fact*, in daily living, there is no comparison. Nibbling other things, however nice, is not the same as tearing and chewing a chunk of under-done half-bloody red meat. It doesn't satisfy, it doesn't generate the same drive and sheer physical energy, or sense of being able to fight anything that challenges you, as does eating meat. Strangely meat has this quality, beyond its ordinary nutritional value, of enabling the eater to develop his full driving-power, both physical and mental – or perhaps I should say psychological. In my life I have known a number of vegetarians, and generally speaking (though here I know I should not dogmatize, for there are bound to be exceptions to the rule) although they enjoy excellent health and long life, they tend to lack great physical energy, personal dominance, and that quality called 'drive'. Why this should be, I don't know, but this is my experience looking around.

Well now, there is meat *and* meat, and butcher's meat and wild meat. To start with, there's red meat and white meat and various grades between, but for me only the first is *real* meat. Beef, mutton and venison are the Big Three. All should be mature, dark, bloody and strong-tasting, fairly hung and underdone in the cooking. The first two should also have heavy rinds of golden fat upon them, because the fat itself is luscious and because you will not get full-flavoured juicy rich meat from a beast that does not carry the fat of maturity. (Venison though, does not carry much or any fat upon it, being a wild meat.) Thereafter meat starts to descend in nobility. Pork however is a fine filler-up on a cold winter day, and bacon is tasty. Poultry is nice, if it's duck, goose or turkey – or a well-stewed barnyard fowl. But the Lord preserve me against those two abominations, veal and battery-chicken. Of all the things which dare to call themselves meat, these come at the rock-bottom of the list. 'White' meat is a travesty of meat anyway, and how honest folk come to waste their money on such tasteless, gutless, soulless apologies for flesh, I don't know.

Further to the matter of modern meat, present-day butcher's meat is but a shadow of what it was. Once-upon-a-time, when local butchers killed their own local-bought beasts in their own back-yards meat was real meat: blackred and luscious, rimmed with yellow-gold fat, the scarlet blood running into the enamel dish beneath. By contrast look into any butcher's shop or frozen-food store today: the joints are travesties of their real selves – anaemic dry pink flesh from which almost all fat has been removed and what scrap remains is a pallid white, and which is virtually scentless and tasteless when cooked. (Why has it become so devitalized? Several reasons, I think firstly the beasts are killed too young. Secondly they are raised under increasing arti-ficially conditions. Thirdly, the meat is no longer 'hung'.)

So to wild meat, game proper, which is for me my staple diet. Wild meat is still real meat, raised on the tangy herbage of moor and field, having still the proper qualities of meat: dark colour, strong flavour, and firmness of flesh. (Who would eat tame meat if they could get venison, hare or pheasants? – not I!) The king of wild meats is venison. Black-red and bloody, it is still what beef used to be but isn't any more. My favourite breakfast is a panful of lightly-grilled venison steak about an inch thick! The next best thing is hare, which is likewise dark strong meat. Then pheasant or grouse – but I rarely get this. Then wood-pigeon which is tasty. Lastly rabbit, and the humble rabbit is what I mostly *do* get, which is a pity, for it is not my favourite meat, being somewhat pale and chicken-like, and the least 'gamey' of the wild sorts. However, it's far better than modern chicken, even I had this as a gift. Only one fault I find in game, and this is the general lack of fat. I love fat, and crave for its richness on a cold winter's morning, so do have to supplement the game with pork or mutton fat got from somewhere, somehow.

One thing in passing, I will say before leaving the subject of meat: that is, the enormous difference I find, when cutting up a carcass, between wild meat and tame. The quality of the bone and sinews of a truly wild animal is like that of steel, whilst that of the tame is soft and easily broken – herein lies a lesson for human health, I think, in these days when we hear so much about injured joints and muscles. The above, vegetables and meat, and just a little brown bread, constitutes my normal daily food and gives me a full and balanced diet. However, just before the onset of winter, in December, I do buy-in extra stores to supplement this should I be snowed-up for any long period. These consist of simple, nourishing things – oatmeal, nuts, raisins, dried apricots, black chocolate, and, if I can afford it, either a can of treacle or a pound or two of dark brown sugar. And of course tea – I can do without it if I've got to, but a pot of hot tea on a cold day does both warm and cheer!

One group of things you will find lacking in my list of vital foodstuffs which most folk think of as indispensable – milk and dairy produce. I have no milk in my diet at all – I keep a tin of milk-powder for friends and visitors – and only very rarely have any butter or cheese or eggs (though I do like the latter). I dislike milk intensely – nasty sloppy cow-juice – regard drinking of it above the age of childhood an infantile practice, and in my heart despise dairy-farming as a decadent occupation. (And now I'm in trouble with those of my friends who are worthy dairy-farmers!) Milk is the most *unnatural* of all food-stuffs, for in Nature no animal drinks milk beyond the age of infancy, and I have never observed it to be in anyway beneficial to a human adult. (If you happen to *like* it, well that's another matter.) Oh, and sugar. Except for the brown treacly sugar which I lay in against the winter, and which I use-up with the rhubarb in the Spring, I have no regular sugar in my diet – my annual consumption is less than two pounds per annum.

Having got food, one has to prepare and cook it, or at least part of it. This I confess I reduce to a minimum, and for two reasons. The first is, evolving from years ago, stark lack of time, or, if you prefer it, sheer laziness. I don't like indoor work, so I soon got to the state of never cooking what I could eat raw, and never washing or refining what I could throw into the pot just as it was. I soon made a couple of wonderful discoveries: how much *nicer* everything tasted with its husks and rinds on, and how my health and vigour improved as I continued with this practice. Next, I discovered that very quick cooking in only a very little water (as distinct from the *stewing* which most folk give their poor vegetables) made the taste even nicer, and what scrap of juice was left in the saucepan when the veg. were 'done' made a nice gravy. So now I eat more or less everything, chopping-up coarse outer leaves of cabbages and stump with a pair of big old scissors, and not even bothering to wash root-vegetables – just brush the earth off them and bung them in the pot! What a fetish some people do make of cooking, washing and refining everything and taking all the substance, taste and nourishment out of it.

As to my opinion of modern, refined, processed, pre-packed, tinned or frozen foods, as you may have gathered, it is nil. Oh yes, some of it is very tasty, and it is no doubt convenient, but in terms of nourishment and sustenance I rate its value low. This devitalized, anaemic foodstuff is the curse of modern civilization (if civilization is the word) being the root cause I verily believe of the ever-increasing modern ills from bad teeth to internal troubles and a lot more as well, including general lack of energy. In a sense it may be called negative poison, since it deprives the body of those elements necessary to combat the ills and stresses of life.

So far as I am concerned, I may sum up my philosophy of food by saying, eat good natural fresh food, eat as much of it raw as you can, what you must cook, don't overcook, and be sure to consume the 'gravy' since it is likely that many vital elements boil-out into the water and are lost when this is drained away. Don't refine anything, use your teeth to tear and chew and grind as Nature intended. Enjoy your food – to take pleasure in it is part of the art of living.

A note on bread to end with. The very nadir of degeneration reached by modern bread, already reduced to cotton-wool, squashy and plastic-packed, I saw proclaimed on an advertisement somewhere the other day: 'Soft White Bread'. So much for Daily Bread!

CHAPTER NINE

Shanks' Pony

ONCE, long ago, I had a horse and could ride any where I wished to go but now I have only Shanks' Pony.

Shanks' Pony is a very good steed however, if you know how to use him and treat him reasonably well. His two legs will take you anywhere that four legs will, and into places where no wheels can get and his running-costs are only a pair of tough boots and a stout stick. He needs to be well-fed and exercised – but then so do I under all the circumstances of hill-country life, so no extra expense in maintaining him!

On this subject of walking, where shall I begin? For me, walking is necessity and pleasure all in one. More than this, it is one of the cornerstones of good health: for I am convinced that the exercise of strenuous walking is beneficial to the whole body and to the mind as well.

Now, from the practical point, walking is indeed a necessity. I chose to live in a remote place far across the moor, with only a piece of muddy lane and then a mile of rough moorland track to link me to a road proper, and beyond this point there's another two-and-a-half miles of lanes and moor-road to take me to the little village and its Post Office which is my metropolis. (A dash to the Post and back is a seven-mile round.) My friends and neighbours of the hill-farms all live from a mile-and-a-half to twelve miles off, away across wild moor, high windy fields, squelching bog and many a rushing stream and precipitous cleeve. So, being unable at the present to afford a horse or a Land-Rover, if I want or need to go anywhere at all, I've got to walk. For me, this is nothing new, as I've lived in the country and walked hard all my life, and in the past twenty-five years of what I may call 'wilderness living' I've become accustomed to walk very long distances over rough tough country in all weathers at all times of day and night, summer and winter alike. This to me has been no hardship, only good healthy exercise, its only drawback the length of time taken out of a day when there's sometimes a lot else to do as well.

Many friends seem to envy my ability to walk long distances over tough terrain, and up steep hills, frequently carrying a heavy pack (though show little desire to emulate this) and often ask, don't I get tired, and such other rather facile questions, so here followeth a dissertation upon walking in hill-country written from half-a-lifetime of experience.

Three things there are that contribute to good walking: good feet, good leg-muscles and good lungs (and heart). Conversely, there are three ways of being tired: footsore, leg-weary and beat, and these usually occur in the stages of this order. If you are not fit, the first parts of you likely to give out are your feet, these extremities becoming sore with the unaccustomed chafing. The second stage of tiredness is that of leg-weariness, the muscles of the legs beginning to feel the strain and ache, and the last stage, that of 'beat' is when someone finds his-or-herself gasping for lack of breath and unable to go on because breasting the steep hills is too much for heart and lungs. Now the remedy for all these shortcomings, and the promotion of proper fitness, is just the very simple one of walking – just that, a little to begin with if you are not used to it, increasing the distance each day, and then not slacking-off when you can walk properly. As with every physical exercise, it must be part of your life if you are to be proficient in it.

For ease of walking, the first consideration is comfort of the foot. 'No foot, no horse' says the horseman's maxim, and the same being true for the walker, one must be well-shod. Now what constitutes being well-shod depends largely on individual preference, but myself, I am unorthodox – I like old Wellington boots. Several sizes too big, and usually split in the foot, there's always plenty of air pumping round your feet, and in really bitter weather there's room for a stuffing of hay or newspaper, which is a much better insulator than all the woolly socks in the world. A propos of this, I do not wear socks in boots at all. I find they swaddle your feet, making them sweaty, they are apt to ruck-up, or rather down, and chafe the foot, and if you get water in the boots they are then soppy and uncomfortable. (Added to which they wear into holes quickly, are time-wasting to darn and expensive to replace.) So I walk barefooted in my boots, with just a pad of newspaper under the sole or wrapped around the foot, which is clean, dry and airy. And my feet? They are like a dog's pads, like leather, the skin of those parts which touch ground so thick and hard that I can run my fingers over them without any feeling at all. I dare to say, these are feet in good condition, able to stand up to anything.

With leg-muscles it's just a case of using them until the muscles are so developed that they will go on endlessly without tiring. With heart and lungs it's just the same thing – use. Though some folk may be initially gifted with better wind than others, it is constant use which develops the lungs and strengthens the heart, and so gives the power to go up steep hills without getting out of breath.

As to what distances one may walk, twenty miles 'at a stretch' is reasonable for anyone who is fit, more if you have plenty of time and can take 'breaks' between whiles. If you have the time an average of ten miles a day is fair exercise for fitness. (When I had more time to spare than I seem to have nowadays, I used to walk an average of seventy to a hundred miles in a week, most weeks of the year.) What speed you go at, is up to you, but for myself I reckon to cruise along at about three-miles-per-hour, taking the rough and the smooth together.

Which brings me to say terrain is a great factor in one's walking. Naturally one can make better time on a hard track than on rough or soggy ground. In this country a short-cut is *not* generally the quickest way there. The old dictum that the shortest distance between two points is a straight line doesn't apply to a land of bog, rock, river and thicket! If getting to somewhere in the shortest time is your aim, rather than rambling for fun, then it is wise to stick to the hard, plain ways. On the other hand, you will tire less over varied ground than on the unyielding surface of a hard road. One other thing which surprises newcomers to hill-country walking is that going *down* hill is as great a strain, and a greater slowing-up, as going up-hill. Until you have acquired the necessary balance and sureness of footing, you are likely to stumble or wrench an ankle if you go too fast. Another thing too, I have found, is the expediency of 'changing your gears' according to the nature of the ground. A long swinging stride is the best for general walking, but when going up or down steep slopes it is natural to change to a shorter-stepped more driving sort of stride, while to cross thick heathery tussocky ground a high swinging action is called for. On smooth level ground you can push on into a running-walk or jog, or for good measure a brisk run, which is a good tonic for both wind and limb.

My companions to walking are a stout stick of ash or hazel, a hank of strong cord, a sketching-case, the usual knife, a handful of oatmeal in my pocket (raw oatmeal is the best thing for staving-off hunger), also a satchel or rucksack if I am going to the village. The stick is not only an aid to walking generally, it is useful for thrusting forward in boggy or uncertain places to test the ground for a foothold. The hank of cord is for tying-up anything that needs to be tied-up – as for instance a gate whose hasp may suddenly come off as you open it (the cardinal sin of the countryside is to leave a gate open) or as a mender to a rucksack whose webbing has suddenly parted company. The sketching things are for making notes with brush or pencil of anything of interest.

The knife, my usual powerful sheath-knife, cuts anything that needs to be cut – and sharpens pencils as well!

One of the things one has to accustom oneself to, if one is dependent upon oneself for hauling supplies, is the carrying of weight. Hence the satchel and rucksack. The best way to turn yourself into a pack pony is to get the weight up onto your shoulders. Once there and well-balanced, off your hands and arms, it is surprising how little one notices a moderate weight and how even a comparatively great weight becomes bearable. So the rucksack is the proper thing, or, failing this, just a hessian sack which, with its contents, can be slung over first one shoulder then the other. Or a Dick-Whittington bundle on a stick is another handy way of shouldering things. (As to how much you should reasonably carry, this depends on yourself and the distance of carrying. Myself, being a small person, I think up to twenty-five pounds for indefinite distances, proportionately more for short ones. I can carry a 70 lb. hay-bale across the 100-yards-or-so width of the average field of these parts.)

In winter I wear or carry a heavy black plastic mac such as is regular wet-weather farm gear round-about here. It is one of the few things that is really waterproof and does not tear easily on gorse and brambles. Not that getting wet actually *hurts* – I think I have said quite a bit about that elsewhere – but in winter being clammy is uncomfortable and the subsequent drying-out of heavy winter coats a nuisance. I also possess a pair of black waterproof leggings, but these I do not wear in ordinary wet weather as they are both heavy and hot, and slow down one's walking. They are reserved against the time of deep snow, when they really are necessary, because without them the snow would work down inside the boots and make a wretched wet mess around your ankles. Oh yes, and a Sou'wester. Again, this is for wear in snow, especially blizzards – it protects the face against the icy blinding stuff, so that with head down you can bore into a storm if you should be forced to face one.

So equipped to face all weathers and most eventualities, off you can go wherever you wish. Having said that walking is a necessity for me, I will now say it is a pleasure also. Walking has so many advantages over other sorts of locomotion. Firstly, I am completely free, north, south, east or west, I can go unhindered by anything. With the exception of a river in spate, there's nothing I can't go over, under, through or round. I am not confined to roadways by a car, nor to having to return to a point where a car is left, as do folk who walk from a car. I can on foot climb rocks or pick my way over bogs where no horse could go. I can stop at any point to admire the scenery and look into the distance, or to sketch, without having to worry about either parking a car or coping with a restive horse.

Best of all, I am close to the ground, near enough to it to see and touch all the things of life, quiet enough to hear all the small sounds of the natural world. Close enough to brush past the leaves and the grasses, tread amongst the flowers, see the small butterflies about them, the dragonflies by the riverbank, the spider on a mossy stick, the beetle on a stone, the lichen on the rocks. Feel the breeze on my face, touch things with my fingertips, put my hand on a sun-warmed rock. Smell the sweetness of the herbs, taste ripe berries as I pick them. Hear the song of the birds, the rippling of the stream, the movement of life in wood and thicket. I can sit down and rest when I want to and gaze on all the wonderous complex patterns of living things. I can run for joy when the west wind sends the ocean clouds high over the moor like sailing-ships in the sky. I can take off my boots and walk bare-footed over short smooth grass and feel the touch of it under the sole of my foot (for the instep remains sensitive where it does not normally touch the ground), like some extra perception. I can wade across rivers, boots under my arm (for experience has taught me that it is easier to dry wet feet than wet boots) and feel the silken tug of the water like a living force about my legs. Or I can sit by a pool and skim pebbles over its surface until I am mesmerised by the silver spray and ever-circling ripples.

Shanks' Pony is also a good little hunter. When hounds come crying down the hill on a cold winter's day, Shanks' Pony follows on too. Again, on foot I am able to go where a horse cannot get, and knowing the country and guessing the probable run of a fox can often keep closer to hounds than can followers on horseback. Sometimes even, I have the experience of being alone with hounds when even their huntsman is hard-put to get to them. To stand alone with hounds and watch them casting and hitting-off the line of their fox for themselves is a thrill indeed!

Last, perhaps the first, of all the benefits of walking is its contribution to good all-round health. Taking one into the open air with vigorous use of the body, drawing one close to the wonders of life, it creates both physical and mental well-being. Long may Shanks' Pony thrive!

CHAPTER TEN

Running Repairs

ONE of the corner-stones of self-sufficiency is the ability to do almost every job yourself, without outside help. Now this means mastering to a certain degree a diverse number of skills and occasionally taking a few risks.

Running repairs come in all sorts and shapes, so to speak, big and little, and almost always the need for them occurs at the most awkward times, generally when one's hands are full with something else and the weather inclement – this indeed seems to be the common denominator. When this happens – I mean several things claiming attention at once – one has to decide which is the most imperative under the circumstances, and give it priority above the others. However, the lesson to be learned is not, if you can help it, to let things get in a desperate state in the first place, but to keep a check on what you know is bound to need repairing from time to time, and to try and do these repairs *before* the state gets desperate and whilst you may have a little time in hand and the weather is fair.

The first thing to come to mind, because it is a vital matter and because it is prone to storm-damage, is roofing. A sound roof over your head is an absolute necessity in this climate of (usually) incessant rain, and roofs as such are very vulnerable to storms. (A childhood memory of the North Devon coast is having our house roof torn off like a box-lid on the seaward side by an Atlantic gale.) So a constant check must be kept for any signs of weakness and leaks and loose tiles stopped at once. It is easier to get up on a roof on a calm dry day and do a bit of fixing than to wait until the height of a gale and then, seeing something tearing loose, have to choose between water pouring in on precious belongings or going out and risking your neck up a ladder in drenching rain and wind trying to save the situation. (Misfortunes will happen though, even after as much foresight as one can command, and I have on one or two occasions had to go out at the height of a winter storm or in the first light of dawn or the last of dusk to try and cope with a situation wherein I knew I was about to lose a part of the roof over my head if I didn't do something quickly. And damned unpleasant such occasions have been.)

Roofs in my world come in a variety of styles and materials, from slates to 'tin' sheeting and roofing-felt – not to mention split polythene fertilizer bags – and ricksheets.

I confess to a dislike of dealing with slates. This is because in most cases (other than low outhouse) a slate roof, whether of house, barn or shippon, is fairly high above the ground and of a steepish pitch necessitating working on a long ladder with a long drop below. Of such a situation, I am not at all fond, especially when working alone. However, when I had a tiny cottage in a lonely combe, I had to sometimes essay this job, though confess unashamedly that I preferred to do it when I had a friend around to hold the foot of the ladder. But by way of compensation, it's so nice when you come down and feel the ground under your feet again!

'Tin' – by this is meant galvanized-iron sheeting – is even more awkward to handle on high, it being heavy and unwieldy, but mercifully I've never had a lofty tin roof to deal with. On low sheds it can be managed easily enough, albeit with a few bangs and scratches and some cursing. There is one thing to be said for tin, and this is that it is virtually indestructable. You can knock it about and drop it from a height, and apart from a few dents it will be none the worse. The same cannot be said for the corrugated 'composition' sheets which so often take the place of other roofing materials on farm buildings today. Just one sudden blow, and the expensive sheet will go 'scat abroad'. As a friend once said, 'If you chuck a turnip at it he'll go right through.' (Why anyone *should* chuck a turnip at it, I don't know, but in these parts where the steepness of the ground is such that often the back roof of a building is below the level of a lane behind it, nothing is impossible.) The usual roofing for small sheds and chicken-houses is 'felt' over board. This, contemptuously called 'tar-paper' by a Canadian friend, is the least satisfactory sort of roofing, for it is fairly expensive to buy and scarcely lasts weather-proof for one year in this stormy climate. It frets, cracks and tears in a very short while, and needs renewing before each winter. I have found a much cheaper expedient is to split plastic fertilizer bags and tack them on like large overlapping tiles. Whilst they last they are 100-per-cent waterproof, and though like the felt their life is short – they too fretting and wearing under the impact of constant storms – their great virtue is that they cost nothing, either initially or to replace.

For the complete weather-proofing of a caravan roof, under which you and all your most precious goods are to live, a 'sheet' is necessary. Now ricksheets can be of all sorts and sizes, and all are very heavy and expensive. The old-fashioned treated-canvas ones are not suitable for permanent duty in the teeth of hill-country storms, their purpose being as temporary covers for hayricks, etc. – I have had several and the proofing has gone out of them in next-to-no time. For permanent use, I've got to confess that the modern nylon-based plastic is the best, being tough and long-lived and completely waterproof. Now one of the arts of being sufficient-unto-oneself is knowing how to handle a large sheet, especially if there's a gale blowing-up, which there usually is when you need to get the sheet into position quickly, remembering that a ricksheet in a high wind has the positive passion to become as the main-sail of a full-rigged ship! The secret is in the rolling: a sheet should always be folded sides to the middle, then the two ends rolled until they meet likewise in the middle. Thus you have a compact 'ball' which you can hump up a ladder, dump in the middle of the area to be covered, unroll so that ends and sides fall automatically where they should, then quickly as possible tie-down one guy-rope at each corner before the wind can lift the whole of it off. Then go round fixing all the other ropes.

Roping-down is an art in itself. You need to have an instinctive sense of tug, strain and tension, supplemented by a knowledge of the ways of the wind plus an appreciation of its tremendous power in exposed places. (Again, I learnt early, on a coast where roofs ripped off like box-lids and ricks had to be weighted-down with boulders.) Just how to place a lacing of ropes and cords so that they supplement each other and baulk the wind, is to be acquired only by experience, but two things must be remembered, firstly, some sort of ropes tighten in wet weather, and some slacken – which does which you find out the hard way – and must be adjusted according to the weather; secondly, if one rope breaks in a gale it must be replaced at once, because if not double strain is put on the next one, and if that goes too, triple strain on the next, so that before you can say 'knife' the wind will have its wicked way and tear your sheet off and into pieces. It's better to curse and go out and get soused, then come in and dry yourself than to lose a roof altogether.

From roofs one descends to walls. Walls can be of all sorts, but the usual kind in these parts are of rough undressed stone set in the fashion known as rag or rubble work. These, if not rendered-over, must be kept 'pointed' or they will sooner or later 'slip' with the alternate rain and frost of a hill-country winter. Usually sooner, as it doesn't take long for the weather to get into this sort of masonry. So one learns to mix cement (the old dressing was lime-plaster, but this doesn't seem to be in use any more) and to patiently fill crevices with a small builder's trowel (handy this, for weeding the borders too) and make a neat finish that is both weather-proof and pleasing.

From walls of buildings one comes to field and garden walls. Most in this region are the construction called 'dyking' or 'ditching', which is really the stone-facing of earthen banks. Parts of these are apt likewise to slip and fall after a bout of torrential rain. Like everything else, this stonework wants replacing as soon as possible before things get worse. The traditional dry-walling is simple enough in principle: you take the biggest stones first, butt them longways into the bottom of the bank, then add another tier above these, and another, etc. finishing with the smallest stones at the top, then capping the work with turves to finish off. But to do it well enough for the work to stand for a score, or perhaps a hundred years against the warring elements and the rasping hooves and horns of beasts is another matter. Still one tries.

Speaking of beasts leads on to 'gapping'. Beasts of the moor, both sheep and cattle, not to mention everything else from ponies to deer, are great destructers of boundaries. Their persistence in forcing a way through anything to anywhere they want to go is remarkable, and might earn them commendation in any competition for effort and determination. Consequently, you must be forever on the look-out for gaps and places where gaps are likely to be made and be capable of mending the same with enough efficiency to snooker the aforesaid beasts. It takes some doing. I speak from experience. Hill-sheep can jump like fleas and crawl like caterpillars, and bullocks will push and shove their way through almost anything by sheer brute weight – except taut barb-wire which is the one and only thing they respect. The art of gapping consists of being able to think like a ewe or a bullock or a pony or whatever the particular reprehensible beast may be. (Have you ever seen an old ewe down from the moor walking with calculating intent along a boundary wall or fence which she wishes to negotiate? She gauges to a nicety the spot where the barrier may be weakest, or slightly less high, before making her leap.) You must say to yourself as you walk along your boundaries (remembering that prevention is better than cure and it's best to stop invaders *before* they are in your garden than afterwards), if I were a sheep, would I think it worthwhile trying to force my way over, under or through this? If so, strengthen the place. Then when mending a gap already made, think as you work of trying to get through it yourself, and work against that idea. As to *how* you stop a gap when you haven't time to do the proper walling, well, I've already mentioned barbed wire for bullocks, but this will not stop sheep unless the strands are laced very close together. You need a length of wire mesh or a piece of 'tin' (unsightly but effective) or lacking these, a bundle of cut thorn-branches. And remember, if you have to drive-in stakes for support, the defending wire and thorn-heads should always be set outwards, on the side the animal pressure is going to come.

Keeping-up a road is one of the offices of hill-country living. In most of the places where I have lived, such road as has given access has been but a track of unmetalled loose stone, mud and grass. Now ground-down stone is one of the best farm-road surfaces you can have, lasting for ages (tarmac doesn't last long at all – it has to be frequently renewed at great expense) if you attend to its needs now and again. The great enemy of such a road is torrential rain. Unhindered, this will pour down the steep gradients as down a stream-bed, tearing gaping washouts in the surface until your road looks as if it had suffered an artillery bombardment. So you have to take digger and shovel and do something about it. Garbed in raincoat, you 'turn the water out', this is to say you cleave gutters in the lower-side of the road-edge at salient points, then pile clats of turf athwart the roadway, so that – with luck – the torrent may be channelled off before it digs holes in the said road. If the damage is already done, then it is best to wait till the rain stops, then take wheelbarrow and delve-out 'metal' or shillet from somewhere and fill the holes up before the next deluge makes things worse. It's effective, and it doesn't cost anything.

Simple carpentry is another useful skill in a life of make-do-and-mend. Often it is necesary to repair parts of a wooden shed, outside or in, and useful to put up shelves etc. – but this belongs to the chapter on making things.

Then there's all the running-repairs about a home proper, to be undertaken once or twice a year. The puttying of cracks around window-frames, the painting of walls and woodwork, inside and out, the creosoting of sheds, gates and fences, and the tarring of weather-ends of buildings. Things must be made thoroughly weather-proof ere the winter storms begin, and as neat as possible before the summer comes.

In all these odd-jobs there is, in the end, a simple satisfaction in the doing. One is dealing directly, by simple means and mechanics with the forces of Nature, using one's own ingenuity and judgement, and this in itself is something fundamental to human life.

CHAPTER ELEVEN

Life's Chores

ALL LIFE has its chores, and so has mine no less than any other. Some I perform daily, or in the week's cycle, or the cycle of the seasons, and each is essential to my well-being and some to my very survival. Yet these are all congenial and their simplicity gives them a dignity of their own; indeed their performance comes to be almost a ritual within the sacred complex of home and garden.

Now all these chores are in their well-doing very satisfying. If they lack the fire of creative work, they are at least quietly pleasing and having done them one has the feeling of something worthwhile accomplished and future comfort secured.

First of all, there's getting up and getting-down to work. I arise early, about 5 o'clock all the year round – well, it's four by Nature's time in the winter if I can manage it – so as to get my quota of writing done before daylight calls me out to the wide world, and my first act is to get a pot of hot tea. If it is winter this means getting the wood stove going, if summer just the little paraffin boiling stove. Then, with tea-pot and

59

mug in my lap and oil-lamp at my shoulder, I settle to work. The next thing, now that I have three bantams (two little hens and a cock) is the 'Tweeties' coming to the door and demanding their breakfast. So a little bit of corn scattered out on the stone doorstep. Then next after that my own breakfast. This is my heaviest meal of the day. Into the boiling-saucepan goes what meat I may have, followed by potatoes and root-vegetables, then when the boiling is well under-way such green vegetables as are in season to lightly steam on top. As I've probably said elsewhere, I don't go in for much preparation of vegetables – just rub the earth off the ground ones and slice them, and rough-chop the greenstuff, tough outer leaves and stumps alike with a pair of big old kitchen scissors, and that's it, into the pot they go.

Breakfast I eat out of the saucepan (it's so nice and hot – why bother to mess up a dish?) continuing to work with one hand and by this time listening to the B.B.C. news-bulletin with one ear. Then to arise properly, make bed and tidy-up – and what an amazing pickle the place has got itself into after the upheaval of the morning's and the preceding evening's pulling-out and strewing-about of books and papers! And what a misconception it is that a small place is easier to keep clean and tidy than a biggish one! The smaller a home the more cluttered up and jam-packed it gets with everything piled one-thing-on-top of another and things inside things and things in front of things or underneath things, until you cannot turn round without knocking something over and starting a chain-reaction which knocks a lot more over, and whatever you want is sure to be underneath a dozen other things, and to get it you have to pull it out and that upsets everything on top, and then you can't get it back into place when you've finished with it, so stuff gets out of order and important things get lost. (Some folk say, how can you possibly *lose* things in one small room? – well I *can*, and sometimes lose them for years until by sheer chance they surface again. On the whole though, I have a sort of mental index of knowing how far down the strata to look for particular things, rather like a geologist dealing with rock-layers.) So tidying-up is somewhat of a major undertaking every morning, but at last it's done and I can look around with pleasure on my tiny home-world with all its bits and pieces back in proper place. Yes, everything has to have its proper place, where it 'lives' and can be looked-for and felt-for even in the dark. The problem is keeping it there.

Next, the morning sweep-up. Shaking the sheepskin rugs, etc., and brushing-up the bits. Here again one meets a fallacy head-on; that a very small place must be easier to keep clean than any other. It is not. Firstly, you can't get round anything to sweep-up or dust-off without, once again, knocking something over. Secondly, there's always such a lot of stuff to be swept-up and dust to be dusted. Where does it come from? I don't know. I can only suppose that constantly turning around in a small space beats up dust and debris whilst the wood-fire does undoubtedly shed a film of fine ash over everything. (Also, when dealing with hay, one brings in 'bits' on one's clothing.) At last the little house is set to rights and I can feel pleased. If the morning should be wet, I can find time to polish up my pieces of brass and copper, to see them smile back at me, and reflect the fire and lamplight glow of the evening, but on a fine day there's no time for such indoor games. The great out-door world calls!

Next, to check livestock. A brisk walk round sheep (in winter this has to be done earlier, at first light) then cattle, counting up the numbers and looking them over to see all is well. There are few pleasanter things than 'looking' over stock on a fine early morning, with all the world waking to life between a blue sky and a green earth and the rising sun touching and moulding the animal bodies. (Admittedly it's not quite such fun in drenching rain, but there, one has to take the rough with the smooth.) Maybe there are strayed beasts to be fetched back from another field and gaps to be plugged too.

Then the garden. Always there's the garden with a hundred-and-one things calling for the doing, whatever the time of year (on my way out to the stock I'll have a quick look round just to see what seeds have come up in the night, what flowers have opened with the morning light, what wonderful things have come to pass in the night's darkness – and alas, sometimes what damage has been done by midnight pests). Such a joy is a garden, full of life all around you, all your own. A vital thing too, for me, since half of it produces two-thirds of my food. So to work at whatever needs to be done this day.

Lunch-break, if fine, sitting in my old folding armchair on my bit of lawn in the sun, contemplating my small flowering kingdom and combe below and the hill beyond. (Lunch is just a mug of tea, a slice of brown bread and what I can find to go with it.)

The afternoon is going-out time. I take my sketching-things, my rucksack if need-be, and set off for a long walk, to the village, to visit farmer-friends, or just to ramble in solitude over moor and bog, by the rivers or the rocks.

Like all things, I come home at eventide, and then there are the evening chores to do – or, if I know I am going to be out late, I must needs attend to these before I go.

Water to be got in. Since the spring does not always function, this often means going down to the stream below. So a couple of buckets and a jug, and down the steep rough slope. Here is my 'waterhole', a tiny rock-pool under the rushes with the glistening rill of water splashing in and rippling out. On a hot summer afternoon the sound of the water is like music, its glitter in the sun silver-gold, and sometimes there are dragonflies, flitting about the dark hollows under the tussocks like blue fire at the mouth of an enchanter's cave. I fill the buckets with the jug, drop the empty jug in one, and clamber up out of the combe. The way is steep, the ground trappy, the buckets heavy – water weighs ten pounds to the gallon – and I am glad when I get safely to the top, for if I slip and fall, then I must go back again for the precious water and struggle up once more. Oh, how precious it is, the shining water, for it is Life – for nothing lives, neither plant nor beast nor Man, without water.

Then wood, enough for two fires, the evening's and the morning's. Small dry sticks to be broken for kindling, logs to be sawn for backing-up. Pleasant work with chopper and bow-saw, brisk and vigorous on a cold afternoon. Stack in what space there is indoors, near the stove.

Then fill the two small oil-lamps with paraffin and clean the lamp-glasses ready for a light against the coming darkness.

Bring in vegetables, fresh from garden, for supper and for tomorrow's breakfast.

Bait the mousetraps, and put in strategic points about home, inside and out, and cover-up to prevent birds getting at them, or more precisely getting caught. (Mice are the bane of my life here, out-doors in the summer and indoors in the winter – they are field-mice and the greatest overall pest I have to deal with, attacking everything from peas and beans in the garden to potatoes in store, and from crocus-bulbs in pots to clothing in drawers.)

Give Banties afternoon feed. Look round to see if anything else needs attention before night-fall.

Now dusk, and I'm home for the night. Light the lamps, lay and light fire in stove. Put kettle on for pot of tea, then frying-pan for supper. Tea-supper is my second hot meal, had anytime after five-o'clock, and my last for the day. It's usually a fry-up, with more meat if I've got it, vegetables kept back from the breakfast cook-up, and plenty of fat.

Relax in front of the fire sitting on my three-legged stool, delight in its leaping flames, eat my good supper out of the old iron frying-pan, held hot on my knees.

Put flat-iron onto embers to heat for bed-warmer (much better than hotwater-bottle, as holds heat longer and can't burst). Then get out sewing-things, retire to bed to recline in luxury like Roman Emperor, listen to radio (if there's anything worth listening too) and occupy my hands with make-do-and-mend needlework until too tired to go on, then read a bit, wind clock and set alarm. Finale, turn out the light – and the next thing it's morning again!

Of periodic chores, washing is the most outstanding, or at least that calling for the greatest effort. On Monday I must get the stove going well and put on pots of water and set buckets outside on the paving-stones, one for washing and one for rinsing (that is, if it is fine, for often I do my washing on a wet day since sunny days are too precious for anything but gardening and sketching). Washing things, kneeling down in the sun to work, is a rewarding task, as they come out so nice and clean as though with new life, and the water is so soft that little rubbing is required. Then pegged on the line across the corner of the lawn, they wave gaily like flags proclaiming home, and when I take them in they smell sweetly of the fresh moorland air. Ironing, though, I don't do – there seems no point in it, since I've never been able to iron one crease out of a garment without ironing two more into it. So long as things are clean, that's all that matters in my life!

Sunday is 'flower-day'. Every Sunday I bring in fresh flowers and arrange them in the earthenware jug by the window to delight me in the early mornings and evenings. I love flowers, and home is not a home without them. Even in winter when flowers proper are over and done, there is always something to be gathered, be it only budding twigs and evergreen leaves.

Also, if it is summertime, Sunday is 'dead-heading' day, when I go round with scissors and nip off the spent heads of flowering plants so as to keep them tidy and still flowering.

Then there are the periodic cleaning jobs. Most important of these is cleaning the rifle. A spread-out rug to put all the bits and pieces on, and he has then to be stripped down and the barrel cleaned, then all the parts well oiled and finally reassembled. It is a pleasant and proud job. Hunting-knife too must be checked to see no speck of dirt is getting through the defences of oil to set up rust.

Tools too must be kept clean and oiled. If possession of good tools is a first requisite of self-sufficiency, care and maintenance of them is the next. Good tools do need care, as much as good guns, though they seldom get it. They need it and deserve it, the first because they will last longer and work more efficiently if looked after, the second because they serve you well and are your partners in life. You owe them that. 'The good workman careth for his tools.' They need a dry corner to live in, and to be cleaned, dried-off and oiled every time they are brought in after use. (This does not take very long if can of oil and rags, etc. are kept by their roosting-place.) It is a personal obligation. Never should the faithful things be left in the rain or out all night. They have their right to a home and care.

Then there are seasonal chores. On summer evenings after hot days all the plant-tubs must be watered (flowers in pots get very dry and

63

thirsty) and extra water got from spring or stream for the purpose. Slug-bait too must be put down under stones for the beastly things that eat my flowers.

On winter mornings, there are hungry beasts to be fed, cattle waiting for their hay, sheep for their 'cake'. As Spring advances I must be out at dawn, carrying the gun, to see the ewes are on their feet and the crows warned-off. Then there is the covering of tender plants at night against the bitter Spring frosts. Of chores there are no end!

And some idiot once said to me, 'What do you do to pass the time?'(!)

CHAPTER TWELVE

Making Things

ONE OF the great virtues of a wilderness life is that it's essentially creative. It has to be. One must always be making things, firstly from necessity and then for pleasure. You make things because you need them, also because the making of them gives you satisfaction and achievement.

On a tight budget and far from the centres of commerce and industry, the simplest way to possess something you want is to make it – that is, if you have the materials and the capability to do so. However, with regard to this, not only do you need to acquire constructional skill, but to exercise ingenuity and imagination, for you do not always have to hand the proper stuffs for the job and so must invent and improvise. Hence the great benefit to mind as well as body in the matter. One of the curses-in-disguise of our modern society is the tendency to buy everything. Well, some things *have* to be bought – one cannot readily make a saucepan or a garden-fork – and some things demand skilled professional craftsmanship in their making. Fair enough. But a host of things there are which one can make for oneself more cheaply and with greater satisfaction than by buying.

One of my recipes for living has always been, 'if you haven't got it, make it, if it doesn't exist, invent it'. In this way I get what I want, in more ways than one.

The things which I make for myself, on dark winter evenings and on days when it is too wet to do anything out-of-doors, are many and varied. Looking out and around my garden I see all sorts of things created from odd bits-and-pieces put together under the shelter of the lean-to on afternoons when the rain bucketed down. My prize creation is the sundial, and this is its story:

It all started with *wanting* a sundial. This is how everything creative and constructional in life does begin. You want something. As I've always said, the two vital things in life are, firstly, knowing what you want, and secondly, knowing how to get it. So, I wanted a sundial – there was a place in the garden that positively called for a sundial – but I could not afford to buy one. So I looked round for materials with which to make it. Then it so befell that one winter evening I was visiting a friend, and as I sat by her log-fire, her son came in with a big armful of bits of old timber from the barn and threw this on the fire to replenish the blaze. On top of this wood I then saw, about to be consumed by the flames, a massive leg of a bit of old Victorian furniture of some sort. Suddenly I saw its potential – the column of a sundial! 'Can I have this?' I fairly shouted, making a snatch at it and rescuing it as a brand from the burning. The prize came home with me in the Land-Rover, and I later set to work on it. It was a fine turned bit of hardwood, beautifully spiralled, and soon with the aid of my faithful tools and some other bits of wood I added to it a cap and plinth, then with an old wax-polish tin I made a dial, then rigged up a gnomon with a piece of odd metal, and finally set it in the appointed place with two bricks as a base. Then I painted the whole with stone-grey paint (except the dial which I did in black with white time-marks) and stood back to admire it. It looked grand, if I do say so myself, and seen from the gate could not be told from an expensive bought one. It still stands today and not only is it a pleasing garden feature, but it serves a useful purpose in that when the sun shines it tells me the time most accurately, if and when my clock has stopped. How did I get it set in the first place? Well, I confess I cheated: 'summer time' having then just come in, I simply turned on the radio, waited for the 'pips' to go for the one-o'clock news, and then set the midday-noon mark under the shadow of the gnomon and fixed it. (Alternatively, I could of course have done it per compass, setting the mark under the shadow on a due north-south axis line.) These rough-

and-ready methods would not satisfy a mathematician, I know, but they are serviceable enough for me!

Then there's the 'bird-table'. Just a small thing constructed of bits of deal, a tray with a neat roof, painted black and white and set on a post just outside my door where it makes a pleasing feature against the space of the combe beyond. Here it draws small birds to a place where I can see them.

Further to the subject of birds, the latest idea/project I have in my mind at the moment is a bird-bath. Being delighted at the antics of a blackbird in a small 'bath' in a friend's garden last spell of hot weather, I determined someday I too must provide my visiting birds with such an amenity. Shortly afterwards I happened to espy a knocked-off hub-cap by a roadside – some motorist having bumped against the bank – and guessing the owner would not come all the way back from somewhere to look for it, I picked it up. The shape was ideal, so gracefully shallow, just right for a bird-bath! I took it home in triumph, sorted-over some cracked flowerpots until I found one just the right shape and size, inverted it, and there was the pillar-stand for my dish! The two shapes make a perfect whole, and now await a piece of putty to seal them and a coat of grey paint for a finish.

The ability to see *shape* in all sorts of odd things is a perception to be cultivated. Once I came across what had been a cowl off a chimney lying in a friend's garden, covered with thick green moss, and its form was just that of a 'Japanese' lantern; I begged it, got it home, and set it up on the angle of the wall. It made a fine ornament and I've always intended to put a small light inside it one night just to see the effect.

Indoors, one of the most useful and satisfying crafts is that of patchwork. A little time spent each evening with needle and thread, and one can turn odd bits of fabric into jewel-like patterns of colour which will make gay cushion-covers, curtains and bedspreads to furnish a small home – and summer skirts to wear as well!

Embroidery is another pleasing craft to adorn a home, I'm no needlewoman, having neither domestic virtues nor social graces, but I'm always promising myself that in the coming winter evenings, I'll enliven plain pieces of material with some brilliant bold stitchery. From a combination of this and patchwork one could make some really splendid wall-hangings; these would have a double value, that of being pictures-on-the-wall and of helping to keep the place cosy in winter. Fabrics and draperies are great insulators against the winter cold – after all, that was the down-to-earth origin of the magnificent medieval tapestries – they kept the cold at bay in the castle hall.

Then there is the possibility of weaving. I collect all the cord off the hay bales, and am always promising myself that I will set up some sort of frame to weave mats from it. I figure out various ways of interweaving bright-coloured bits of stuff so as to make bold patterns. But I've never actually got down to the job, as I've always had plenty of skins for rugs about my home.

Few things there are that give a greater richness, a sense of barbaric splendour to any room, large or small, than fine skins. They are the oldest, the most natural covering in the world for floors or couches or for walls, or I suppose for human clothing itself. The curing of skins is surely the oldest craft in the history of mankind, and one that certainly comes under the heading of 'making things'. My small dwelling-place is full of skins of all sorts, from sheepskins on the floor to pelts of deer, fox, hare, rabbit and calf draped more or less everywhere, all of which I have cured and dressed myself. But I have already said much about this in a previous chapter.

Progressing from skins, one can also home-cure other trophies such as slots and brushes, just soaking them in a mixture of salt, alum and paraffin.

Then there's the dressing-out of a fine head to set on the wall, if you are lucky enough to get one. This is in fact quite simple. You put the skull in a pan of boiling water over a hot fire, suspended so that the antlers are not themselves immersed, then just keep things going until all the flesh is boiled-off and the bone white and clean. Trim off face-bone below eye-sockets, also nose so that it will set nicely against the wall, finish-off with a stiff brush and hang up – and your abode is tuned to a baronial hall!

Another basic craft is that of simple carpentry. With a few tools and lengths of timber one can set up shelves and make all sorts of useful bits-and-pieces. From there, you can go on to carving supports for shelves or figures for ornament. There's no end to the craft of woodwork.

Arising to art proper, if your walls are blank, paint a picture to fill the space. Get an old frame, paint this a suitable colour, then cut a board to fit it, and paint whatever you like on it! It's so much more fun than buying (and good pictures, even prints, cost an awful lot) and painting is really very easy. Or, you can paint a motif directly onto a wall or side of furniture. The simplest way to do this would be to cut a stencil from a piece of card or something, but this should not be difficult. But with wall-art it must be remembered that either the painting and its background must be washable, or you must resign yourself to having to blot-out your decoration next time you need to clean or paint your walls.

Then there's sculpture. The urge to have and to make symbolic sense-delighting figures is great. Get clay or wood or soft stone and model or carve forms and shapes. I've made all sorts of figures of clay or wood in the past, though not as yet employed stone. Small figures of animals and riders-on-horseback to enliven a shelf, plaques to adorn a wall; and I've always *intended* to get around to something bigger, but time is so short. There is something curiously compelling about three-dimensional art, whether it's small painted model figures or large bronze or marble heroic statues. Sculpture is particularly telling and forceful out of doors. Figures moulded by the sun and casting shadows on grass or wall. Heraldic beasts boastful on gate-piers, a graceful statue by a pool or half-revealed in a woodland glade – but these are dreams, for me at least.

Simpler more practical garden features in my way of life are tubs and dry-walling. One of my chief constructive occupations of the winter days is to collect all the old buckets and bowls I can lay my hands on, and bash holes in the bottoms and paint them green for plant-tubs. Lengths of old board I fashion into troughs. Sometimes I let my imagination go a-wandering off into ideas of modelling bold ornament on the surfaces, such as I've seen on coveted stone or lead cisterns – but so far I've not had the time to experiment with this.

Simple low walling, steps and pavement are necessary to a garden in these parts, the first because of the need to hold back earth on a steep slope, and the last to make a dry footway across ground that is mud for half the year. Stepping-stones soon suggest patterns, whilst walling, which can be of so many sorts, starts a train of mind that leads on to pillars and arches and God-knows-what-other flights of fancy. In next-to-no-time one is back to Art again!

Oh, if only there were more time to a day than a brief twenty-four hours! For of things to make and do there is no end and life itself is all too short for the adventure of living.

H.L.B.

CHAPTER THIRTEEN

Old Wives' Tales and Some Modern Fables

THE world is full of fables, despite our being supposed to have out-grown the age of superstition. Old wives' tales die hard, and as any one of them does finally depart another takes its place, so that we today are no more free of these than were our ancestors.

We may not believe in witches, curses, and the wearing of green as the harbinger of ill-luck, but we – that is, the majority of modern folk – do believe whole-heartedly in a lot of other fallacies.

Now most of the superstitions of today are those concerning health, and seem to be accredited even by doctors. I say, most of the cherished beliefs of the health-and-hygiene-conscious folk are fallacies, and this I dare to say out of my own experience over many years.

I come, though, to the point of speaking upon the subject of health

70

and vigour, my own that is, with some hesitance, for it is well known that boasting brings trouble on the head of the boaster – this is one of the moral texts of the ages. Yet in fairness to all things, truth as I know it concerning my own well-being over the past years must be told, even though I draw the spite of some vengeful force upon me tomorrow. I can only say that, during the years of my wilderness-living my general health and strength have been remarkable. Barring accidents (sprains and torn ligaments) and one or two emotional upsets (as when some favourite trees got cut down) I can truly say I have never been ill. I am never ill, never have colds, never go to a doctor, always have abounding energy, possess considerable muscular strength, while all my senses are keen to the point of pencil-sharpness. I eat like a horse and sleep like a log, and wake before dawn with zest for the coming day. That's the plain truth.

Those of my friends and acquaintances who live in conventional comfort with such modern 'amenities' as central heating and refrigerators plus all other mod-cons, and have all the usual coughs and colds, and all sorts of other ailments from indigestion to arthritis (and sometimes worse ills) seem envious of my health, the more so as they cannot understand it and say it would kill them to live as I live. Having said that, they then rush off to fill themselves with pills and potions and harry the poor overworked doctors.

Now herein lies the seed of the truth, I think. Such good health as I have is attributable to the very fact that I do live a rough tough life. Modern Man is destroying the natural good health that should be the inheritance of all by what I would call negative living. More and more of superfluous comforts, processed foods, neurotic fear of illness, morbid passion for hygiene, and less and less of physical exercise, fresh air, fresh food and positive enjoyment of life.

For myself, I have found, generally speaking, the harder one lives the healthier one becomes. The more coddled and less dynamic, the weaker one grows. Overall, I know not a better maxim for health than the old one which says 'Work hard, play hard, eat well and sleep well'.

Concerning the wide gap between my way of living and that of my friends, and of my state of health and theirs, I have from my own personal experience over many years (plus my observations of other folks' disabilities) long come to the conclusion that almost every accepted precept of health is erroneous. Most of what we are taught to believe is just a mixture of 'Old wives' tales' plus modern medical fallacies.

So now, I will start by attacking a few fables. Of food: it goes without saying that food is itself the very stuff of living, and upon what one eats depends one's whole structure of life, health and growth. However, as I

71

have written much concerning this in a chapter devoted to the subject. I will confine myself to reiterating just the few facts that are outstanding on the controversial level. Here follow some common fallacious beliefs:-

Firstly, that if you eat rough coarse food you will get indigestion. Rubbish, and a complete introversion of the facts. Unless you *do* eat roughage you most certainly will suffer from indigestion and other complaints as well – it is for this reason, to wit the eating of over-refined foods, that the majority of people suffer the bane of indigestion and allied troubles. Myself, I eat every sort of husk and peel that I can chew and tear, and my inside is in perfect order. Likewise rough-stuff is necessary for your teeth. Gnawing and chewing is absolutely essential for the maintenance of good strong teeth. (A great deal is talked about bad teeth, especially in children, these days, and all sorts of chemical remedies put forward, but I would unhesitatingly say, the cause is soft refined food – give the kids something they can chew and tear, and their teeth will be O.K.)

Next that fat is bad. Nonsense. All my life I've been a heavy fat-eater. Fat – real, honest animal fat, beef, mutton or pork – I regard as essential for the withstanding of winter cold and for the maintenance of full physical vigour. Fat does not make you fat (I weigh just eight stone) nor, in a person leading a normal life, does it do any harm to the heart. I can go up the roof-steep 1,400 ft. hill the other side of my combe full-tilt without stopping for breath, whilst younger folk lag behind. What fat does is to create heat and energy in the body.

After this all manner of fallacies. That fried food is bad. Well, all my food that is not boiled is fried, and I've lived half of each day of my life on fried tack and thrived on it. Fried food is good rich food, giving good sustenence with plenty of nourishing fat.

That salt is bad. The reverse is true. Salt is a vital ingredient in food, especially in hot weather. Anyone doing strenuous work or exercise, particularly in summer, needs plenty of salt with their food for the simple reason that in sweating you lose salt, and therefore must replace it quickly. If you don't believe me, then next time you've done something vigorous, lick the perspiration on your arm and see how salty it tastes!

That everything with mould on it is bad. Not so. Most moulds are harmless, some are very beneficial (is not penicillin a mould?) Of my own food, what is not eaten absolutely fresh is eaten with mould on it. I have no means of keeping stuff, other than a small meat-safe on a cool wall, so when I do get anything in bulk, it just has to repose there, or hang up, until I've eaten my way through it – by which time it is often blue, black, white or yellow. I've eaten much of my food in this state from bread to meat – especially the latter – and it has never done me a pennyworth of harm. After all, you eat blue cheese, and consider it nourishing and nice-tasting, don't you? So why be pernickety about other things?

That water is only fit to drink if it comes out of a tap. It is amazing how many summer hikers call at farmhouse doors for a drink of water! (This according to my friends.) Yet they must have passed by a hundred springs and rills of water – that is, if they have really come across country – on their walk over the moor. Either they don't recognize water when the see it in Nature, or they think every drop of it has been deliberately poisoned! Well, I live on a mixture of spring water, rain water, and sometimes river water, and I've never had anything the matter with me. I remember this past hot dry summer having to go down to the larger stream at my boundary gate for water, the nearer stream having got so low as to make filling a bucket difficult, and a friend visiting me during one of these water-hauling operations. She commmiserated with me saying 'So much hard work, and then the trouble of boiling it all . . .' I said I hadn't time to mess about boiling it, I just used and drank it as it was. 'Oh', she said, 'but supposing there is a dead sheep anywhere upstream?' I replied, 'Dead sheep be damned, I know where there's a dead cow'. Somehow I don't think she enjoyed her cup of tea much after that, though this was boiled! As for me, theoretically I suppose I should be full of typhoid, brucellosis and liver-fluke – but all I can say is that if I am, it does me no harm! Which brings me to comment on the modern preoccupation with excessive hygiene. In my opinion, the more you seek to evade 'bugs' the more prone to them you become when you do meet them. You build up no resistance to them, and are therefore liable to be knocked flat by any that you meet suddenly. Of course there are some bugs that are pretty deadly, I know, but on the whole a well-nourished body should be able to cope with most. I've come to the conclusion that hygiene has probably killed as many people as it has saved, so mostly counts itself out.

That getting wet is a source of coughs, colds and general illness and that wet feet in particular are disastrous. Just rubbish. I've been soaked to the skin many times over, and most days of my life I have wet feet – I habitually wear old Wellington boots, the toes and heels of which often gape like crocodile's teeth, and I live with cold muddy water squelching in and out. I never get colds, etc. Anyway, the whole theory is crazy: people wash and bathe, don't they? If that doesn't give them colds, why should any other sort of wet?

That sitting down on wet ground leads to illness. Again, rubbish. I sit or lie on sopping wet ground many times when out sketching, and get up wet through to the skin – and I've never been a penny the worse for it.

That the wearing or putting on of damp clothes or sleeping on a damp mattress will be the cause of serious illness, and that damp conditions generally are the root-cause of rheumatism and arthritis, etc. Not true at all. I've often worked out-of-doors all day in soaking wet clothes, had to put them on wet next day for lack of being able to dry them overnight (anyway, the best way to dry-out heavy clothing is to put it on yourself as on a clothes-horse and go out into the wind) and I've frequently donned half-dry underclothing when I needed said raiment and it wasn't dry from washing. Also, I've sometimes had to sleep on a squelching mattress because I've come home after an absence and found the roof had been leaking over my bed. Well, not only do I not get colds, but I haven't got an ounce of stiffness in my whole body. The truth is, damp and wet never did anyone any harm. What does, is undernourishment (not eating the right sort of food) and worrying about oneself. I'm prepared to make a guess that such ills as 'screwmatics' are due to a failure of diet somewhere along the line.

That draughts in a home are bad. The reverse is true. A current of fresh air is necessary in a house at all times. To swelter in an unventilated room is unhealthy. I myself always have a cross-draught of clean air right across my litle dwelling-room, arranged by having the window on one side open a space and the door on the other also wedged open a little, no matter what the weather. Thus I always breathe fresh air and am refreshed by it.

That night air is bad for you. Again the reverse is true. There is nothing so healthful as sleeping under a wide open window, nothing so refreshing as to wake up in the morning and feel the sweet dawn air on your face. The window by the head of my bed is never closed, and the first thing I do if I stay a night at a friend's house is to open the window there – I would feel claustrophobic shut in away from the fresh night air.

That hot baths are good for you. I've never thought they were, least of all the very hot sort in which people soak themselves for what seems like ages. Such a sort of boiling must draw the natural oil out of the body, also soften up the sinews. A quick shower-bath is much more healthy, I'm sure. Anyway, when I have a conventional bath at a friend's house, I see it is never more than luke-warm, and I don't stay in it longer than necessary, and on getting out I always throw open the bathroom window so as to let the cold fresh air lick my body dry – you can't get briskly dry in a steamy atmosphere, no matter how hard you rub. (Yes, I know the Finns, who boast of their health, have hot steam baths – but traditionally they do what the English don't – run out and roll naked in the snow to counteract the effects.)

That cold is bad for you. Not so. Cold is bracing and invigorating, stimulating you into moving briskly, indoors and out. I've often sat down to sketch amid snow and ice until my hands and feet were quite numb, then run hard to restore the circulation – and felt fine. At home, on winter nights I let the stove go out before I lie down to sleep, and on waking often find everything freezable turned to ice and hoar-frost glinting on the walls. So long as the body is well-fed and well-clothed, one thrives on cold. The modern system of central-heating is the most pernicious form of heating ever invented for a temperate climate; folk swaddle in their overheated boxes, never opening a window, while the germs proliferate in the stale air, and wonder why they get ill. *This* is where 'colds' are caught and infection flourishes. I've always noticed the incidence of illness tends to be highest where there is central heating.

That exertion is bad. The greatest fallacy of all. Vigorous physical exercise is one of the cornerstones of health. It is lack of it that leads to so many ills. Few people use their bodies sufficiently. Man as an animal is geared to a life of physical energy. Proportionately as he does not use this inborn energy (and perversely he seems to be forever trying to avoid bodily exertion of any sort) he becomes unbalanced and a prey to many evils.

The same is true of the mind and spirit. So many people worry, seek to avoid challenge or hard work of any sort, restrict their interests, then so often break down anyway. They seem oblivious to the fact that the human mind, like the body, is geared to accept the strain of danger and striving, and they do themselves no good by the avoidance of it.

One hears much of 'breakdowns' nowadays, and full hospitals, and the taking of drugs, but I do not believe that breakdowns are really caused by overwork. I do not believe that any one ever died from overwork – but I think many come to a bad end from *underwork*. That is to say, from lack of using the powers and urges inside oneself. There is one devil that destroys: Frustration. Failure, disappointment, disillusionment, heartbreak – these are the evils that lead to sickness of mind and the aggravation of the ailments of the body.

Therefore I say out of such experience as I have had, strive to lead a full life, one of positive living, with the powers of body, mind and spirit as fully developed as possible. (So many folk seem to follow a negative path, just accepting the second-rate without fighting for anything better.) Try to do more things, not less. Don't take pills and don't worry about health – the harder you use your body the heathier it will become – just eat well and sleep well. Enjoy life, especially the simple physical side of it; the closer you live to Nature and natural things, the healthier and happier you are likely to be, and the more zest you will have for all other things. Try for yourself!

CHAPTER FOURTEEN

Lending a Hand

SOMETHING which one learns, and learns early, in a country upbringing is to be a useful person. Now I am not implying that people who live under other circumstances are not useful, nor that they are unhelpful by nature. Rather it is a case of their skills being from the force of those circumstances mechanical and specialized, also because surrounded by public services of all sorts from Fire Brigade to R.S.P.C.A. they are seldom called upon in times of emergency to do more than lift a telephone receiver. In the country, and in particular remote hill-country, where many miles often separate one farm from another and the forces of Nature must be daily contended with, self-reliance in all manner of situations is a necessity and help to a neighbour in difficulties an obligation.

So one learns from childhood onwards to do all sorts of basic necessary things and to cope with a variety of happenings. To ride a horse, to shoot, to drive a tractor, to handle livestock, to make hay, to carry corn, to lamb a ewe or wrestle with a calving cow, to tie a fleece or mend a road, to beat out a bush-fire or dig through snowdrifts – these and a score of other things are essential accomplishments. You do all these things as a matter of course, to help yourself and to help your neighbours, for as I've said, helping a neighbour who is in any sort of difficulty is part of the way of life in a community of hill-farmers.

So one lends a hand. If, in going about the country you see anything you know or suspect is not as it should be, you do something about it. A swinging gate, not tied-back, should be shut and a boundary-gate most especially should always be shut. If you see a ewe on her back, you get her up. If you see cattle or sheep where they should not be, then you do something about it, either directly or by going along to report to the owner.

Then if a neighbour is laid low by illness or has to be away for some unavoidable reason, you or someone else must step in and do the chores – check the stock, milk the house-cow, shut up the hens, and, if it is winter, feed-round the beasts.

Chiefest and most usual of commitments, though, are the seasonal peak-times. Having wrestled with your own affairs, if you then have time over, you help a neighbour who is short-handed. These high-tides of hill-country life, at which an extra helping-hand is most appreciated, are in their usual sequence: lambing, shearing, dipping, haymaking, harvest, gathering (ponies or sheep off the moor), cattle-testing and ear-tagging, and root-lifting. Such is the stuff of hill-country farming.

All these things are part of my life. Each year brings to every one here its cycle of work and life, struggle and harvest. The first of these festivals of work, if so they may be called, is lambing. This, in a pastoral economy is a vital time. On the lamb-crop depends the prosperity of the farm for the coming year. Here in the hills the traditional month is April, though the first lambs usually start to come the last week in March, and the latest in May. This is late according to lowland reckoning, but then this is a late country, with never grass enough to keep stock until early May, and perhaps not even then. Now comes three weeks day-and-night work for each family, with a rota so some sleep whilst others walk the endless rounds. Everything about the farm is geared to this great festival of birth. Every possible building has to be turned-out and strawed-down and divided into pens to give shelter to the new-born for their first night on earth in rough weather. The kitchen stove must provide hot water all the night through and about it cluster tall cardboard boxes for the reception of weakly lambs, whilst table and dresser fill up with a clutter of feed-bottles, syringes, and all manner of veterinary medicines. Folk eat and rest when they can, and every extra 'hand' is welcome, but no 'visitors'. No-one ever goes visiting at lambing time unless it is to help.

One lambing after another I remember through all the years. Fair, fine weather sometimes; storm, howling wind and driving rain, perhaps snow and ice at others. But always the ewes gathered near the farmsteads in their hundreds, their bleating filling the air, the sound soon to be joined by the higher-pitched plaintive voices of new-born lambs. The endless tending, the struggle for a life when a birth is bad, the night-rounds with storm-lantern playing along hedges and away into space, casting its eye of light onto the hunched forms of sheep and sending black shadows away behind them. The wonder of new life, the misery of pain, the wretchedness of mud and splashing wet, the joy of the sun rising for a fair day. Then the fields filling with gambolling white lambs on Spring-green grass like a living Easter-card. From generation to generation of Man and beast, the cycle of birth, life and death, and life again.

Next, as the year moves on, comes shearing, and anyone who can 'tie wool' is in demand. Again the memories of many a shearing: the barn full of racketing machinery, the baa-ing of sheep, the smell of wool. The mid-summer sun beating down on the roof, shearers, tiers, catchers and sweepers all streaming with sweat, the salt sweat running into your eyes and dripping off your nose, the seemingly endless repetition of movement like a stylised ballet. I tie, one fleece after another, throw, roll, carry to table, tie four-square, chuck up onto ever-mounting mountain of fleeces at the end of the barn, then back for another – it is hard to keep pace with fast shearers. Occasional breaks to the cask of beer or cider in the corner. Then the blessed pool of silence as the engine stops and someone calls 'Dinner'. The shearing-dinner – oh what a dinner! The farmhouse kitchen crammed with men, the long table loaded with a whole ham or turkey or quarters of mutton or giant round of home-grown beef, plus every sort of vegetable, followed traditionally by bowls of strawberries with lashings of cream. Gossip and laughter, then back to work, and then another mighty meal, tea-supper, to finish with.

Then comes haymaking, a time of immense importance and utmost work. On the hay-crop depends the winter well-being of all the stock. Such a time of anxious watching the weather. Even in these days of quick-baling hay can be ruined by rain at the last moment, just as it's ready to carry. (In fact more hay is spoilt or lost, I would say, by relying solely on mechanical methods than was when hand-labour made cocks of it – but that's another matter.) But the fine hot days of hay-making-these are the ones I like to remember. The July sun blazing into the field, the heavy scent of the hay almost over powering in the heat, the throb of tractors, the shouts of folk. Loading in the midday heat, heaving the raw heavy bales, sweat soaking my shirt, myself standing higher and higher on a big swaying load, struggling to bond the bales well, for your life depends on it if you are going to ride home on your load. Then the journey to the barn, high up with a wonderful view, but having to duck to avoid the sweeping branches of trees en route. Then unloading and stacking the bales in the barn, muscles straining to cracking-point, and the heat under the roof stiflng as you near the top. Load after load, until someone calls 'Tea'. Oh blessed word! – and we all throw ourselves down in sun or shade as of choice with hay-bales to lean on. Jugs and mugs of hot tea, sandwiches, scones, biscuits and cakes galore – with always a luscious chocolate-cake for the high-spot – talk and lots of fun and the dogs trying hard to call attention to themselves. Then on until the dew begins to fall, and with luck we have finished the field.

After the hay comes harvest, though often not until September or even October in these parts (and I have known corn carried in November some years). Not all the hill farms in this region grow corn nowadays, but many still do, and by corn is meant oats, for the climate does not favour wheat or barley, though a little of the latter may be drilled. Harvest hereabouts is still of the traditional sort, with sheaves in stooks and stitches and loads carried to rick or barn on waggons (albeit trailers behind tractors now) for the 'oaten-sheaf' is the ration for bullocks in cold mid-winter, fed whole upon the ground. As soon as the corn is cut, there's always a call for help – sheaves to be stooked, windmowed perhaps if the weather is bad, then carried in. All these simple jobs, the oldest in the long tale of agriculture, call for degrees of skill. To set up sheaves in stooks so that they will stand, to make tower-like windmows so that they shed rain and do not slip, to pack sheaves so that they will ride home in a swaying load – these things are learnt only slowly over the years. Many a load of corn I've made, standing on the swaying waggon catching and turning the sheaves as they come flying up off the picks, setting them heads-inward in a bond that runs first laterally then longways, always remembering that the middle must be kept up, convex-shape, never allowed to sink hollow-wise else half the load will push-out on the way home. Fresh ripe straw is slippery stuff and a badly-made load will soon shift as it rocks down rutty lanes. I've even loaded in the dark when rain threatened before tomorrow's dawn, and it is a dangerous job where you can see nothing but the occasional glimpse of men's heads in the tractor lights far below, and the big load sways under you as it moves on (a good load must always sway – there is something wrong with it if it does not). One works by blind feel and instinct, knowing that one step too near the edge … But I love corn-harvest with its golden glory, its heady scent of ripe grain, the long day's work in autumn sunshine under a blue sky (if one is lucky) and the triumphant sense of 'Harvest Home' when the last sheaves are stacked under barn and tallet roofs. 'All is safely gathered in' – the bullocks will not starve this winter. Deep and atavistic are the feelings inspired by sheaves of corn.

The last of the harvests is that of roots. Since swedes and turnips are commonly 'eaten off' in the field, this means potatoes. Most farms have a 'rap' of spuds down one side of the root-field for the house and for feeding to pigs, and since potato-picking is no-one's favourite job an extra hand is always welcomed as the more hands there are, the less of the work for any one person.

It's a back-breaking and tedious job, and since it falls at the end of everything else, usually in November, the weather is apt to be cold and raw with a finger-freezing wind. However, spuds are good food for man and beast, so no-one grumbles – at least not very much!

Sometime between these high-tides of work, there will be 'gathering' on the moor, to round-up and bring home ponies, cattle or sheep, for sorting and attention. This is real Wild West stuff, gloriously exciting for the young and strenuous for the less-young. Every hand is welcomed, riders on horseback, neighbours in Land-Rovers, children and dogs to run on foot. Early morning on the high wild moor, a strategic dis-position of forces, then driving, doubling-back, hounding onwards, everybody shouting, dogs barking, Land-Rover horns hooting, horses snorting, bullocks bellowing, sheep baa-ing, hooves, charging everywhere – a good time is had by all, except possibly the beasts to be gathered up – until stock is on the way to home-pastures. If hunting is the image of war, then herding is the image of hunting!

Other occasions when extra help is welcome are sheep-dipping, cattle-testing (for T.B. and Brucellosis) and ear-tagging of calves. At all these ceremonies the beasts fight like the half-wild things they really are, and the bovine affairs tend to be like a compound of rodeo, bullfight and circus. Dealing with powerful, either terrified or angry beasts, you need all your wits about you and to have a fair knowledge of the psychology of animals. So far I've survived!

Then comes winter and the long task of feeding the beasts until Nature sends the grass in Spring. The help of anyone who will feed-round on outlying land, or at home when through illness or accident the owner cannot, is greatly appreciated. So, I do my bit here. On winter mornings I feed the cattle and sheep and check them, here on this lonely ranch-farm where no-one lives but myself, and feel myself one with the life of the hill-country.

Rewards? One does not look for rewards for doing what a neighbour should. Yet they come. For me, the right to shoot or fish. A lift to town on market-day. A day at the County Show. The present of fat pork. Goodwill all round.

So we live in the hill-country, neighbours helping each other.

CHAPTER FIFTEEN

Pitfalls and Dangers

'AREN'T you ever frightened?' is one of the questions most frequently asked of me by folk who lead less independent and out-of-the-way lives than mine. To which I answer honestly, No. This they find hard to understand, for their minds imagine all sorts of dangers and horrors likely to beset a solitary dweller in the wilds. So does my mind – and that is why I stay alive and whole!

To be forewarned is to be forearmed is an old saw, and like all such is full of truth. He who foresees danger, calmly and with due appraisal, is equipped to deal with it, and being able to deal adequately with it (one hopes) is freed from fear.

The two qualities or attributes outstanding, as most necessary for a wilderness-life, are sensible attitude of mind and the practical ability to tackle troubles when they come. Since in all things mind precedes and governs matter, let us look first at that.

If you set out to live a wilderness-life, then you must first look the hazards full in the face. Alone, without means of communication (such as phone or metalled road) too far from your nearest neighbour for shouting or signalling (it matters not whether the distance is one or a hundred miles in this context) then you are indeed on your own. You may break a limb or sprain a joint, get hurt in a dozen other ways, or poison yourself by eating the wrong sort of mushroom, and no-one will know anything about it until perhaps yor are dead. You may be faced with every sort of danger from having to get up on a roof in a gale to stop the rain coming through a storm-torn hole, being knocked down (and trampled on) when handling cattle or horses, skidding with a tractor on a wet slope, or having to struggle with a building on fire, to dealing with an escaped convict or a lunatic on the loose.

Having looked all this in the eye, so to speak, you then see that though all or any of these desperate things *may* happen, there is in fact no reason why they *should*, and indeed they may not occur at all. Knowing the dangers, if you at all times act sensibly, keeping one eye open for the particular risk inherent in a specific job, you should not come to any harm.

Beyond this, the element of risk as such is present in all life, and it simply has to be accepted. If you are going to refuse to take any risks at all in life, then what is your life going to be? You are going to end up not daring to get up out of bed. Furthermore, there is no great salvation in playing safe: you might stay in bed to avoid all the dangers of life, and then be crushed by having the ceiling fall in on you!

So, I look forward with zest to life, live it to the full in whatever is my chosen path, learn to judge between a necessary calculated risk and a stupid unnecessary one, and beyond this know I am in God's hands and trust to Him.

Now to look at the practical, physical aspect of the matter. First of all, I *am* alone, and everything that happens around me, I must cope with alone, be it killer-dogs attacking sheep or a bush-fire threatening to engulf my abode. So I know I must be capable of dealing with everything that crops up just as it comes. It goes without saying one must be physically fit and without 'nerves'. Wilderness-country is tough country, hard and cruel beneath its cloak of beauty, country where the black birds come down and pick the eyes out of living sheep who are sick, or where a human being lost on the moor may lie dead for weeks before being found. (Note: this last is not an exaggeration, it happened once not a mile from where I live, a few years ago.) There is no place for weakness when face to face with Nature as it really is and not as the sentimentalists imagine it to be.

The first step in coping with eventualities is to remember prevention is better than cure, but, should accidents happen, knowing how to deal with them is the next. So, a few hints from personal experience over the years.

The commonest injuries one is likely to sustain are those of minor cuts, bruises, sprains and wrenches incurred in daily life. A modicum of these is inevitable in the course of a rough, vigorous life, but unless you are very foolish, none is likely to be serious. Nevertheless, one or other *can* be nasty if you do something stupid. The sprained ankle is the most likely hazard in this country of rough ground and admittedly I've done it several times over. It's so easily done – just a false step amongst the rocks, or a quick turn on uneven ground. The worst occasion was some years ago when I was rambling up the valley, amongst some rocks in a side-combe and foolishly jumped from one stone to another, slipped, and buckled my foot under me. It was bad – and I had to limp and crawl three miles home. When I eventually got back I had to cut my boot off (luckily it was a very old one) and next morning I couldn't put my foot on the ground. However, I tied it up fairly tightly with some lengths of materials and hobbled about, and in three weeks time or thereabouts it had mended and I was charging round again as usual. To this day I don't know whether it was just a bad sprain or whether I broke something. Which brings me to say, so long as nothing is displaced, a sprained joint or cracked bone will heal of itself without any sort of treatment in about three weeks.

The next thing to beware of is wrenching yourself whilst heaving about heavy weights. When lifting anything weighty, first jack it up on a half-way step and then bend your knees and get it on your back, as high on your shoulders as you can, and rise with it *straight*, legs apart, taking the strain on thigh and stomach muscles. Never twist. Alas, I did the latter thing once: heaving a hay-bale over a fence I slipped in the mud and went down with it, twisting my back. I thought I was never going to stand up again! Luckily, this time I was only a few yards from home, so was able to crawl indoors onto my bunk. Once again, I decided that what I had done was to tear some ligaments down one side of my body and that my spine was not itself injured (I having a fair amount of veterinary knowledge). So once again I just tied some 'woollies' around the injured parts for comfort and strapped them tight with a belt, and just went on trying to crawl around. But it was worse this time, because one's back is the centre of one's mechanical being and the pain was excruciating. Luckily a friend came in the next day and I was able to get her to tell someone else to come in and feed the stock whilst I nursed my injuries. She wanted to get a doctor, but I would not have this, knowing my injuries would heal of themselves, and so I just lay there, heaving myself up twice a day for the necessary chores of life, and again in three weeks time I was well and heaving hay-bales about.

On the subject of hay-bales, there are two other ways in which they can be dangerous: in a stack or hay-barn they must never be allowed to develop an 'overhang' else they may suddenly cascade onto your head and break your neck – a hay or straw bale can weigh anything up to 70 lb. Also, loose strings can catch the toe of your boot very easily, so tripping you up – and if this should happen on the edge of the stack, well, that's another way to break your neck.

Concerning ropes attached to livestock, never put your fingers in a loop – if what's on the other end gets ungovernable you may get them crushed. Always hold the rope so that you can release it by simply opening your hand.

Constantly using knives and edged tools one has to guard against cuts and gashes. Knives have to be kept razor-sharp else they are of no use, and indeed a sharp knife is less dangerous to one's fingers than a blunt one – the reason for this is that only a light pressure needs to be put on an efficient knife and therefore one uses it with a controlled motion. With a blunt one, you strain and slash and eventually do yourself a mischief. This goes for all tools in general – if they are efficient you use them in a proper manner, if they are not, then you tend to use force and they buck back at you in some way (and this last is often precipitated by your getting cross with them, which is no state to be in when handling anything potentially dangerous).

Incidentally, all farm implements are dangerous things, from pitch forks to scythes, to say nothing of tractors, and one should always be careful with them. In this case though, the danger is usually to someone else. (The pikes and glaves of the medieval soldiery were little different from the pics and slashers of the peasantry – the general failure of peasant revolts was due to lack of discipline rather than to inferior armament.) So be extra careful if you are working with a friend – both of you damaging him or him damaging you!

Timber presents one of the greatest hazards to the person working alone. Most of the accidents I've known to farm-folk have occurred whilst felling trees and laying big hedges. Standing timber is so deceptive. A young tree looks so airy-fairy waving its light branches in the breeze. But the weight of the trunk of even a young sapling can be bone-crushing. It's so easy too to get trapped by sweeping branches and then caught by a swivelling deadweight limb crashing down at an unexpected angle. So don't act without thinking when felling timber! And don't, when using an axe, wear soft-toed boots – if you have a pair of steel-toecapped boots, put them on, because sooner or later you are going to strike an old nail or something embedded in a treetrunk, and the deflected axe-head is going to bounce off onto your foot – and a cloven hoof is not desirable in a human-being!

Another thing – when chopping and splitting sticks for the fire, if you are in the habit of either banging them on hard ground or smacking them across with the back of the chopper to hurry the job on, as you do so put your free hand across your eyes: sticks so bashed will fly as though catapulted and can hit you viciously in the face.

Then there's the matter of ladders. Going aloft on a tall ladder, whether to fix roofing or to saw off overhanging tree-branches is always a risky business. See ladder is firmly bolted in the ground and resting steady before you go up. Once up, don't lean sideways to the point of overbalancing – it's better to spend a bit of time coming down and moving the ladder along than to end up in hospital. Always lay the ladder down when you're finished the job in hand, or take a break, for a ladder caught by the wind can come crashing down and do great damage to something, perhaps you. Always keep it under cover in a dry place, so that rot will not set in, and periodically examine the rungs for woodworm.

By far the greatest all-round hazard to the lone person, indoors or out, I would say, is fire. Always one must be on the alert about this, especially during periods of dry weather. Indoors, using oil-lamps or stove, one must always watch them. If I have to go out even for just a few minutes I turn out stove or lamp. (It's easier to strike another match than to put-out a fire.) Also, I take care that loose papers of any sort do not fall or blow across the chimneys and ignite. With matches, I see that a spent match-end is always put down on a metal tray or lid. On the whole, though, paraffin is a fairly 'safe' fuel in that it does not give off inflammable fumes. It can only be 'lit' by direct flame-contact.

A wood-stove that can be closed up is a safe fire, but even so you do not take risks. Be careful not to feed it with wood that 'spits' and *should* a spark shoot out, follow it up at once and see that it is *out*. A wood-burning stove gets very *hot*, so keep anything inflammable well away from it. Also, beware yourself of burns and scalds – pots and pans are always hotter than you think.

Remember, in the event of anything catching on fire indoors, the quickest way to put it out is throw a heavy rug over it – no fire can burn without air. Also, for further precaution always keep a bucket of water handy.

Out of doors, never light up a bonfire in dry weather, in a wind, or near a building at all. A sudden gust of wind can carry sparks whirling in the air to drop into a woodpile or into an open door of a hay-strewn loft, and there they can lie smouldering until perhaps the middle of the night, when the whole thing can blaze-up beyond hope of control. (Charred paper is especially dangerous, as it can sail bird-like for long distances on an air-current.) Above all, never risk getting a spark near a full hay-barn or rick – once started, a rickfire cannot be put out. I've seen a hay-barn on fire first-hand, and two fire brigades could not put it out.

The heat was unbelievable, and all they could do was to spray water onto the adjoining roofs to stop it spreading.

In this country of rough moorland, the great hazard of dry weather is that from bush or heath fires, and in this case it is less a matter of what you do as what some other fool does. But of this more in another chapter. Sufficient to say, when confronted with the horror of a wind-driven fire encroaching on your territory and threatening your home, it's no good being frightened – you've got to go out and meet it and try to beat it back. You must tie green branches together and try to turn it back on itself by attacking along its advancing line with non-stop beating.

Other dangers to keep one eye open for are, in a gale, don't walk close under the eaves of a building – slates and sheets of tin torn off by the wind can suddenly descend on your head with a slicing force that can kill you. Beware too of wind-torn branches crashing around.

In time of heavy rains don't try to ford rivers in spate. The little sparkling stream of a summer's day can be turned in an hour into a coffee-coloured fury by a thunderstorm high on the water-shed, and will make no bones about sweeping away a horse and rider, let alone you on foot.

In time of snow, do not go out in a blizzard unless you absolutely have to, and once the stuff is down, don't blunder into fresh snowdrifts. They are too soft to bear your weight, and you will go in – perhaps ten feet or more – and may get smothered. If the snowfall is very deep, stay near home for three weeks, by which time the drifts will have 'packed' under their own weight and you can walk over the top of them. And always carry a spade with you, so that you can dig yourself through or out of an awkward place. Also remember snow sliding off roofs has force enough to break your back.

When bitter frost binds the earth to iron, beware of skidding on patches of ice or wrenching an ankle in the frozen hoof-holes. About home, spread ashes or loose hay on the paths where you walk the most – else these soon become like skating-rinks.

Most of all perhaps, you need to keep your wits about you when feeding livestock, particularly cattle, in mid-winter. They are ravenous, poor creatures, and on foot and alone it is difficult to keep them at bay whilst you carry and spread the hay for them. Apart from being directly pushful, they are apt to charge each other out of frustration, and in doing so may knock you down. Being trampled on by a herd of bullocks isn't a nice thought.

So, having learned, as I've said, to differentiate between a calculated, necessary risk and a stupid unnecessary one, I just remember that famous British saying: 'Trust in God and keep your power dry'.

CHAPTER SIXTEEN

Wild Company

'DON'T you get lonely, so far away from other folk?' is another of the questions I am frequently asked. To which I answer truthfully that I am never lonely, and further qualify this by giving three reasons. Firstly, since I walk a good deal I am seldom out of touch with my neighbours.

Secondly, I have far too much to do to have time to be lonely. Thirdly, when one lives as I do, face to face with Nature and in the midst of wild country, one comes to be conscious of other forms of company than that of human kind. To all of which I would add, that until a person can be good company to themselves, this person is not fit to inflict his or her company on anyone else.

To enlarge upon the first. From here where I live, my neighbours' habitations are from one to many miles distant. For me, accustomed to walk everywhere I want or need to go, at a general rate of a mile in twenty minutes, or three miles-to-the-hour (though sometimes I am slowed down from this average by very rough ground or head-on winds) this distance is little enough, and a brisk afternoon's walk will take me to any one of a dozen friendly farmhouses for an entertaining gossip. Added to this, during the summer months when days are long and weather fine, quite a lot of my friends from further afield come to see me here. However, during the winter it is true enough to say that I see few people, for the days are too short to go far from home on an afternoon's walk, and not many friends care to come up here in the stormy weather and squelching mud of the moor. So then I may go a long while without seeing anybody.

As to the second, my life is so full with so many necessary, interesting and enjoyable things, that I have no time to consider whether I am going to see anybody today or tomorrow or any when. You try crowding into one day writing, farming, gardening, shooting, hunting, studying wild-life, making notes, sketching, painting, making things, doing running repairs, plus keeping your little household going and doing enough of sawing wood, cooking, sewing and washing to keep yourself alive, also trying to find time to read books, write letters to friends and listen to the wireless in the evenings! The hours of the day are just not long enough – there are no minutes to waste on such things as yourself and being lonesome.

Then comes the third and deepest state of things. When one lives alone with Nature, one comes to be aware, gradually and intensely, of the presence, the personality, of everything around you and of a bond, a kinship between you and it. An awareness that every created thing is intensely *itself*, whether wild beast, bird or plant, rock or stream, and has being which is fellowship to you.

Of such company, that of animal life is the most readily to be understood. We being ourselves very near physically to the animals of the earth, and they to us, we can feel close to them as persons. Beloved dogs, cats and horses become almost our other selves, sharing our daily lives like members of a family, and are true company. (At the moment of writing I have none of these, though I was brought up with all three and have loved many dearly, but I do have three Bantams, and they are as near human as anything with feathers on it can be.) Those others of domestic stock such as are dependent on you – cattle, sheep, poultry, etc. – also hold places close to your own life. In their very dependence on you, you are bound to them. They look to you for their food and well-being and you must care for them and in so doing you come to feel their presence around you and to know many of them as individuals. Also they know you, watch you, keep an eye on you and your habits as much as you do on them and theirs, and come to your call. (My cattle and sheep know all there is to know about me as far as their own interests are concerned!) 'A man and his beasts make a man and his home' was said once by someone, and how true it is.

Then come the creatures of the wild into your world. Shy denizens of the Kingdom of Pan, they venture into your domain emboldened by the garden's promise of food. Birds of all sorts, small animals such as field mice, voles, shrews, weasels, stoats, hedgehogs, young rabbits (unwelcome), lizards and snakes, whilst out on the hill the larger and more wary beasts – foxes, deer, the occasional hare, sometimes a badger – look inwards at you.

Life in a wilderness country is indeed a delight to any would-be naturalist. I can spend as many minutes of the day as I have to spare with field-glasses watching all the life that goes on around me. Birds in all their diversity with their incredible marvel of flight reward the nature-lover most of all, whether soaring in space, flitting in the bush or coming to the bird-table. The ravens barking overhead, plaining down the hillsides or tumbling in play, the buzzards soaring on motionless wings, the kestrels seeming suspended on threads as they hover in the sky, the flash of a merlin above the fern, a heron fishing in the stream below, the missel-thrush singing in the ash-tree, the redstarts who have made a nest in a crack of the barn wall, the tiny wrens who creep along the garden fence – all these and so many more are all about me.

Smaller than the smallest of the furred and feathered creatures but surpassing them in numbers are all the countless hosts of insect life, beings of both sun and shadow, at home in every nook and cranny, I do but brush through the heather or turn a stone and there is sentient life from the glory of butterflies to the scurrying of spiders and of ants. The ground itself holds a phantasmagoria of living things. The whole earth pulsates with life, each and every tiny scrap of it intent on its own business, unconcerned with the affairs of Man except when these intrude upon it. An incalculable host of unnumbered beings. Man is but one species amongst them all.

So I keep company with all the creatures of a world beyond my own, yet of which I am myself a part and they my neighbours too.

However, I do not encourage the wild things (apart from putting out crumbs for the birds in hard weather) to come close to my home. In a life such as mine it is necessary to refrain from making pets of them. With a few exceptions they are apt to take too great a toll of my garden-plants. Also, I have to kill a certain number of them – some for the meat I must have, some for the protection of my garden, and some, such as foxes and crows, for the protection of the sheep. Life is a ruthless business, and the law of Nature so often to kill or be killed. The creatures of the wild are best left to the laws and ways of the wild.

Yet with all their diversity and untold numbers, the animals of the earth are only half its life and living company. Perhaps only a fragment of it. Vaster still, all prevailing, are the legions of the nations of plants.

They clothe the earth, lichens upon the rocks, grass in the meadow, shrubs on the hillsides, tall trees in the valleys, making kingdoms of green and flowering life wherein beasts and men may also live. So wonderful are they in their incredible diversity, their marvel of form and growth, their sheer loveliness born of simple need, that often I find myself kneeling or sitting amongst them, speaking to them. Yes, I talk to plants and touch them with my fingertips, and I am certain that in some way they perceive and their being flows out to me. (Why should this be considered such an extraordinary idea? It is true plants do not possess the brain and nervous system of animals, but in all other ways, from the growth of cells to the principles of heredity, they have life like unto our own – why should we say in our arrogance that plants do not feel?) The company of plants is a real and wonderous thing, and I am ever conscious of it.

Deepest of all lies the earth and the sleeping gods of the earth that are the foundation of being. The hills that rise as immutable presences, potent with strange strength, the streams and rivers that flow down from them, dancing in fair weather, storming in wrath in times of rain, singing, shouting, to me always like voices day and night. The pools that lie in the hollow places, dark in the shadow or reflecting the sky as a mirror in the light. The rocks that break from the hillsides like mighty dragon's teeth or lie in strange forms upon the ground. The very stones of the lane whereon I tread. These too are in some way my fellow-beings. Called inanimate, yet they have Presence, Being, Personality and I can speak to them, ever aware of each one of them.

Over all, under all, lastly, perhaps firstly, comes the awareness of *place*. Of this, what shall I say, since it is beyond conscious thought, indefinable by logic, inexpressible in words? Only that some corners of the earth have of themselves an intensely powerful character, something that is a sum total of all within yet more than that. The Ancients felt the emanation of this and called it *genius loci*. As I come home to a beloved place, I am aware that for me this place has in some way become a Presence, a Personality in its whole self. As I pass under the branches of its trees, lift my eyes to its skyline, hear its little stream tinkling amongst the rushes, not only do I salute it, being aware of it, but in some unfathomable way I know It is aware of me, and knows me and welcomes me. More than this I cannot say.

Loneliness does not exist in solitude.

CHAPTER SEVENTEEN

Blanket of the Night

WHEN day is done Night casts her blanket over all things for rest until the morrow's light. How beautious, how wondrous is the night when star-studded or moon-lit, how deep in mystery when velvet-black with darkness!

One of the strangest of things to me is how so many people shun the darkness, whilst some seem actively afraid of it. They will not go out at night if they can help it (except in a car) and if they must, then they carry a torch which they point at the ground the whole while and keep eyes upon that beam before their feet, and never look upwards at the Heavens.

In their homes they have blinding electric lights, which they turn on early and keep on late, and have as many going at once as they can. Even if they sit by a real fire or, at the other extreme, have the 'telly' on, they still have that abomination, the overhead central light, right in the middle of the ceiling, of the greatest power possible, glaring down on them all the while. Its merciless stare mocks both the ancient magic of the fire and the modern marvel of the television, and penetrates into every corner of the helpless room (into which no-one wants to see anyway) destroying every atom of cosiness and killing the essence of home. Even worse, comes the appalling fixture of strip-lighting, which makes everything and everybody a pallid, shadowless yellow-green. (So great is my aversion to this, that I shall include it in a Chapter of Hates in some future book.)

Worse, if people come into the country from suburban areas the first thing they seem to do is to put a great arc-light outside their front-doors and illuminate the whole unhappy area with a glare that takes them right back to suburbia. Even campers, pretending to rough it in tents, will light a powerful 'Tilly' lamp and set it high and wide before the tent to affront the night.

Likewise, in just country villages all the fashion now is for street-lighting which goes on before dusk and stays on until almost (if not quite) dawn. On one occasion not long ago I spent a night at a friend's cottage in a very small Devon village and could not sleep for the glare of a street lamp right in the little window – I cursed and twisted and turned and tried to bunch the curtains across its beam, but to no avail against its remorseless eye which continued to leer at me – if I'd had a gun, I swear I'd have shot it out. (Just what good such illumination does, I don't know, for I'm sure street-lighting in a country area causes more accidents than it prevents, for, speaking personally, I once wrenched my ankle badly over a curb in the distorting light-and-shadow of a street lamp, which I would not have done in the natural darkness.

In all things modern Man seems to hate the night, and seeks to banish it. But in doing so, he does himself an injury for night is Nature's benison after day's striving, the blanket for quietude, rest and sleep, and sleep is the nurse that gives us renewed strength for tomorrow's joyful life and work. Without the blanket of night there is no relaxation, no deep refreshing sleep, no reawakening with pleasure to another dawn. Well, the night-light lovers reap their own reward, for they lose part of their sight, that which we call 'night eyes', becoming blind as bats in the darkness but without the bats' radar-sense.

I welcome the night as it comes to close the day, relax in its gathering dark, finish up the chores and prepare for the pleasures of evening at home with a fire, soft lamplight, supper, books and the radio. Snug in my own little world it wraps around me and soothes and comforts me. My oil-lamp gives a soft mellow light, enough to read and write by, and the firelight dances on the walls in a pattern of brightness and moving shadow. I would hate the hard soulless glare of electricity here in this tiny home. When I am too sleepy to go on with my evening's occupations I turn out the lamp and sleep with the night wrapped around me.

I am accustomed also to being abroad in the darkness of night when occasion demands. If I've stayed late at a friend's party or gossiped too long in the village on a short winter's afternoon, then I must needs come home in the dark up narrow muddy lanes, over rough moorland tracks, and sometimes over pathless pastures, tussocky cleaves and squelching patches of marsh. I never use a torch – such is not only useless, but a hindrance, for like the more powerful street-lamp its beam distorts the contours of the ground. Having lived all my life in mostly rough country, I have learned that the best companions to a night-walk are a stout stick and your own natural senses. Very few nights are truly pitch-black, and unspoilt eyes can see quite well, or well enough, most times even when there is no moon, and if one is accustomed to walk much at night, then one does undoubtedly develop latent instincts. I have found that I seldom bump into or trip over anything – I seem to have acquired, or perhaps just not lost, a perception of objects near to me even when these are unseen in the strictly visual sense. On a more down-to-earth level, if you really can't see the ground at your feet, then just feel it with the stick and the flat of your feet and look *upwards* – the tops of the trees and hedges are always distinguishable against the night-sky and these will give you some idea of your whereabouts. Also, listen for the sound of little rills of water by the side of a track, or the more distant sound of a stream, for these too will guide you. Ears will tell you as much as eyes on a dark night – or in the daytime as well. However, I do, if I can, fix my late comings and goings for a moonlight night, as this makes things easier and more pleasant. In winter I find my life governed to a considerable degree by the moon-periods, as was, I suppose, that of primitive man.

Night hath many faces to its darkness, from those of glory to those of fiercest storm.

There are nights of moonlight when the Silver Goddess rises into a velvet-dark sky and peers from soft-edged clouds upon the sleeping earth. Silver radiance floods the alleys of the night, black shadows under trees are pools of mystery and all the world is another realm from either day or night, commonest objects transfigured to enchanted forms. Sometimes the moon is a new thin sickle, half-way into a pale sky before the sunset glow has departed – one should always wish upon a new moon, bowing seven times before it – sometimes it is round as a disc like a great lamp hung in the sky to see one on the home-ward way. Sometimes it has a halo, a rainbow right around it. Not always is it silver – sometimes it is gold, sometimes rose-colour, sometimes at its rising blood-red. At waning it is pallid, a morning moon fleeing before the lord of the day, the rising sun.

There are fog-bound nights when hill mist wraps the heights and fills the valleys and nothing at all can be seen in the strange luminous darkness. Unless one is sure of one's ground or on a known track, it is not wise to be abroad on such a night, for the blindness of fog is worse than the blackness of night itself, and one will soon be lost (if one *has* a light it will only make things worse – the stronger the light the more opaque the wall of mist before you – as many a motorist with not the wit to turn off his powerful headlights has found). It is on such nights as this that one may see the phenomenon known as 'the Brocken' – a huge shadowy figure rising up before you. I have seen it more than once. (It is of course the figure of yourself projected onto the mist or damp atmosphere by some sort of light behind you. If you don't realize what it is, then it certainly has the impact of the uncanny.)

There are summer nights, soft and warm, when the long green twilights prevail and there is scarcely darkness at all before the glow of dawn heralds another day. There are winter nights, iron-hard with bitter cold, so long and dark it seems that morning will never come again.

There are quiet nights, when no breath of wind stirs and the silence is itself a dimension, with only the murmur of the stream and the cry of a night-bird to break its spell.

There are nights of storm, when the storm-gods seem loosed upon the land with all their hounds of Hell. Battering gales off the Alantic, tearing, screaming across the hills, flaying everything in their path. Rain out of the blackness of night so ferocious that it drives you almost double if you are forced to face it. Howling wind and streaming flood. Crashing thunder and lurid lightning coming close. And one wonders if one will ever get home tonight!

Most fearful of all, nights of blizzard, when the driving snow comes out of the north and all things seek shelter and cower before it. Bewildering drifts mounting up all around you. If one can see at all, all one can see is a savage wall of white out of blackness, bearing down on you with death behind it. On such a night no one should be out at all, and it is better to sleep on a friend's floor than to be so foolhardy as to face a night-blizzard. Then get back if you can in the morning!

Most beautiful of all, the starlight nights. When the sky is clear and velvet-black and the ground beneath your feet is crisp with frost, there are the stars to light the firmament. Their lamps are myriad, their light upon the earth softer than moonshine. I stand, as I have so often, in my little garden under the hills, midway between return from a distant farm and entering the door of my own little home, and I gaze up in wonder at the glory of the stars. The Heavens glitter with their uncountable number in innumerable constellations. Some are large like pendant lanterns, some so small they are but pinpoints of light. Here is the Plough forever wheeling round the Pole Star. There Orion's Belt girded about the hunter. There Sirius, brightest star of them all, there Mars, the Red Planet.

'The Heavens are telling the Glory of God ... What is Man that Thou art mindful of him?'... I am alone with the Universe and with myself, and perhaps the two are in the end but one.

H.L.B.

CHAPTER EIGHTEEN

Household Gods

HERE in the sun of a summer's morning I sit on my doorstep and look both outwards and inwards on my little world. Outwards to tubs and borders full of pretty flowers – pansies, pinks, sweet-williams, roses and Cape-daisies, with marigolds and dahlias to come – and a small lawn just at the moment neatly mowed. Inwards to the sun shining through the windows onto all the crowded things that together make my tiny home.

Of all the things within that I see as I look over my shoulder, there is not one that I could bear to part with, for each is in some way part of my life. All, in one way or another contribute to my well-being, though few have value as men set value upon things in this commercial age, and some are worthless according to monetary standards. But all are dear to me.

In a home-life as small and self-contained as mine all the things of daily life become infinitely precious, entwined with my own being on every level and in every phase, dear companions of the days and years.

All are precious, because most have a vital part to play in the maintenance of life and because every one has some association and sentiment interwoven with its being. Some are strictly utilitarian, some just small adornments to living. Some have been hard-saved-for and bought, some presents from friends, a few companions from childhood. They are themselves friends and if any one were gone from its accustomed place, I would miss it, and feel not only its practical lose but its presence.

Here are my kettles, two copper, one iron and one aluminium. They are the givers of hot drinks and warm water for washing. The two coppers glow and gleam, reflecting sunlight, lamplight and firelight alike, things of joy as well as use. The biggest, Big Brother, has followed me from a childhood home, the other, Small Brother, with pretty fluted lid, was given me off a cottage rubbish-dump many years ago, blackened then, now restored to shining elegance. Small Brother takes time off in late summer to hold flowers by the front window – for a bunch of sweetpeas and heather, or orange and gold marigolds, look their best in a copper container. The smallish enamelled-iron kettle I found lying out on the moor minus a lid, thrown away I know not why or by whom, but still watertight. I brought him home, gave him a coat of black enamel, fixed him up with a lid and sat him on the stove – and there he still is The quick-cup-of-tea aluminium was the gift of a friend, now departed this life, and I think of her each time I use him.

Nearby is my faithful iron frying-pan, which fries me all my suppers plus occasional quick breakfasts. It's a fine heavy thing rescued from a friend's dustbin, into which she had dumped it simply because she had bought a slightly larger one.

On the little shelf behind the stove sit my three saucepans, a big one, a little one and a middling-sized one. These have been bought at various stages of my life and boil respectively stews, rhubarb and eggs.

Another friend from childhood, a heavy flat-iron, stands below. No, it doesn't do any ironing, I've no time for that, its mission in life is to get hotted-up on a cold winter evening, to be wrapped in an old woolly and be cosy at my feet in bed – it's better than a conventional hot-water bottle, for it can't leak and holds its heat longer.

Beside the stove stands the big brass poker that shifts glowing embers for me on winter nights. This too, belongs to far-off days. (Of the wood-burning stove itself, the core of my home, I have already said much elsewhere, so here take it for granted.)

Then there is the small oilstove, just a little boiling sort that I can use to get a quick pot of tea for visitors and for myself when in a hurry. It is old, it needs careful handling to get it going, but it works and it's a friend.

On the shelf beside my bunk-bed stand the two oil-lamps which give me light in the long dark evenings, making a nest of brightness in the immensity of the winter night – a tall brass one from time beyond mind and a very little one, a present long ago, once stripped red, now worn to plain glass.

Then my small earthenware tea pot, also a one-time present, cracked a bit now, which has given me hot tea twice a day or more for many years. The four mugs, different sorts, each a present from a different friend, dedicated to different purposes – one for tea, one for coffee (when I can afford it), one for dipping-up water, one for visitors. Some assorted plates and dishes, again each one with a history of sorts. Spoons, a fork and knife beside them.

Over on the far shelf sits 'Grandmother' my mother's mother's big tea pot, handsomely gilt, used on 'state occasions' when I have several visitors at once. Also some pretty cups-and-saucers inherited from an ancestor more lady-like than myself.

Facing me, an old loud-ticking clock, telling me the passing time. Unreliable, but a friend, as are the others that don't go at all but ornament odd corners - two presents from friends, one bought with the proceeds of a successful flutter at a local race-meeting, so I can't bring myself to get rid of them. Also, carried about in my satchel, 'Ticky' a little old watch, once saved-up hard for, then dropped and stepped-on by a bullock, mended by a farmer-friend who liked to play around with clocks on winter evenings, only one hand now, glass stuck in with glue, but still reliable for about eight hours.

Near to hand a precious old radio-set and a smaller transistor, the one having given me twenty years of faithful service, the other fourteen years. Each was saved hard for those years ago, and together they still bring me all the news of the wide world and are my companions of the winter evenings – the big old battery one is still the best for good music.

And books – books of all sorts, all round the place, some bought, some presents, all of them 'windows on the world', knowledge and enter-tainment of every kind between their covers.

A pile of maps, of Exmoor and of the world, to take me travelling in the time and space of my imagination.

Pictures on the walls, some my own paintings, some framed calendar and Christmas-card ones, making windows for the mind. An earthenware jug on the windowsill which always holds flowers, and at Christmas-time has fir-branches in it in the semblance of a Christmas-tree.

The pair of fine bronze candlesticks in the likeness of dragons which were a 21st birthday-present, and hold ceremonial candles at Christmas, Candlemass and Easter. And some other much-loved little ornaments too, filling corners.

Several pairs of scissors, each serving a purpose according to size, together with all manner of oddments, and pencils and pens where I can reach them easily. Two torches, useful on winter nights and early mornings.

Old field-glasses in a battered case hung by the door ready to hand for bird-spotting. By them the one-time army map-case serving now as a very useful sketching-case, waiting to go out on my next expedition.

By the door too the bucket of life-giving water, the box of logs and kindlings, the can of paraffin and its 'filler'. Before the stove the three-legged stool, on which I sit to worship the fire on ice-cold evenings.

A bird-calendar, two years old, but so nice I can't bear to take it down. Gay tea-cloths, presents with bird and animal designs, too nice to wear-out, so spread in ornamental fashion.

Tin boxes of all sorts everywhere, all sizes, holding all sorts of things from matches, tea and oatmeal to paint, brushes, MSS and hoarded sketches, each recognizable by its distinctive pattern and shape.

Trophies and skins all round the walls and on the floor, each one a memory of a sporting occasion. Five hunting-knives, and the guns in the locker with the cleaning-tack which goes with them. The trout-rod lying long against the wall, its little green box of flies beside it.

My bunk itself, comfortable with warm rugs and blankets and gay with its patchwork cushions.

All this and so much more, from the needles and thread in a little felt pocket to the old pigskin folder holding letters and addresses. Each and everything part of my life, an essential to living and a personal friend.

Individually, each of these things has a 'personality', collectively they make Home. When I come in at night, here they all are to receive me. Each one in its accustomed place, they greet me. They welcome me, promise me comfort and pleasure for the night. They are more than the stuff of physical living, they are companions to life.

How this should be, since they are 'inanimate objects' I do not know. Yet it's so. Sometimes I find myself, child-like, talking to them, and should I break or lose any one of them, I mourn it for a little while as a lost friend. Each Thing is itself. If it has not life in the biological sense, it has presence. It is Itself not the object next to it, and in this sense has Being. Yet it has more than this, though beyond this words cannot go.

What makes it so, that an artifact becomes a Personality? Is it that the craftsman as he fashions an object puts life into its being? Or do we in handling infuse life of ourselves into it? I do not know, but this mystery of creation, the oneness of the spirit of Man with the substances of the earth was wellknown in ancient times. Once, a craftsman finishing a work would inscribe his name on it together with the words *me fecit*. The work of his hands has become a Thing of itself, proclaiming 'this craftsman made Me'. And does not Genesis tell us God created Man from the clay?

So all my simple things are dear to me, and help to make the pattern of my life, and my life would be poorer in more ways than one without them. One of the sad affairs of modern life in general is that things are bought only to be quickly used and then thrown away. There is no time for caring or feeling so that in the midst of affluence there is poverty of emotion and spirit. In this, we are the losers.

Perhaps only the child playing with its toys still knows the truth and realness of Things.

CHAPTER NINETEEN

Neighbours and Excursions

ONE OF of the greatest pleasures of hill-country life is that of friendship and neighbourliness and knowing everybody. In a hill-farming community everybody knows everybody, and everyone is known as an individual – that is to say, a real person.

In so wild a region and so scattered a community any meeting with a neighbour or visit of a friend is occasion for gossip and the putting-on of the kettle for tea. The sharing of news and the giving and receiving of hospitality is part of the way of life of hill-farming. When your neighbour's homestead is a dot in the wide wild landscape, sundered from you by deep valleys, a meeting is an event to be enjoyed!

Where the space and spirit of moorland country still prevail and the farms are islands of life in a world of windswept hills, people and places go together. Each farm is a place in its own right, and its people belong to it. The place establishes you, and you proclaim the place. The farmhouse kitchen is the core of life.

So, visiting and gossiping are the highlights of life in these parts, and news flows freely. For me, living so far out and not having the benefit of the daily post, the particular highlight of my week is the Friday walk to the village. Each Friday midday I take up my satchel, rucksack and staff and set out on the seven-mile round to Withypool to post letters, collect mail and get my weekend loaf of bread and anything else I might need or be able to afford.

If the weather is fine, then it's a most enjoyable walk out over the moor, down the hill to the old packhorse bridge, up the hill the other side to another stretch of moor, then down a long lane and into town! (If the weather is beastly, then it's not so nice, but I always go unless there's deep snow – only a blizzard stops me.) This small village which is the metropolis for these parts is a most pleasant little place of some thirty households, with sturdy-towered church, an inn, and a post-office-stores for a focal-point. Our Post Office is more than just a shop – it is a village institution, a social centre, where people meet people, a place where gossip is exchanged, messages left, parcels collected. Which brings me to say, Friday is gossip-day-in-chief for me as well as mail-and-shopping day. En route and on return my way lies by several farms and so, taking in village homes as well, I'll probably call on half-a-dozen households and perhaps gossip with twenty or more people. So I come home with all the news and talk-of-the-town as well as bread and letters!

Friday however is not the only day of gossip-sessions. All the summer days I see folk more often than not. On my afternoon sketching-and-rambling expeditions I call on one or other of the hill-farms in my circuit and when the weather is fair friends come to visit me. (Sunday is the usual day for fellow-farmers to go visiting because it is the one non-working day of the week.) Why do some people from afar think that I must be *isolated* just because I live where I do? I'll wager that in my way of life, living here in the wilds, I have more friends and meet more people than does the average dweller in a city. It is only in mid-winter, when the days are too short and the weather too bad for long expeditions that I am truly alone, and should heavy snow set in might be cut-off and not see any one for weeks or perhaps months.

Having got settled down with a cup of tea, what constitutes news in these parts? Firstly of course those things which govern our lives. The weather, the affairs of farm and garden, market-prices. Incidents concerning cattle and sheep. Hunting. Household affairs. The iniquities of the Min. of Agric., and other government departments generally, with special emphasis of the lunacy of the local Council. Children, youngsters growing up. Engagements, weddings, births. Accidents, and occasional sudden death. Who is moving from here to there, and who is coming into their place. A new face in the neighbourhood. And scandal! Oh yes, there's always plenty of that and one bit or other is always the *piece de resistance* of any conversation. (And don't say only women gossip – that's a libel – just get two men hitched-up one each side of a gate, and they'll talk till the cows come home.) Crime too now has its place in the local repertoire, for in these days of fast cars and an influx of outsiders from less homely parts, all sorts of wrong things go on that never used to occur.

As to the general circulation of news, we have a wonderful system of communication know as the Exmoor Grape Vine. It is indeed the most knowledgeable, trustworthy and efficient of its kind in the world, or so I am convinced. It seems to work on a combined basis of some sort of radar, telecommunication and extra-sensory perception. It not only flashes items of importance and general interest almost instantaneously around the area, it often knows what things are going to happen before they actually do, and what certain persons are going to do before they know themselves. In this it has a very practical value. It will communicate the sudden illness of a person on one side of the country to friends on the other. It will also give advance notice of any pernickety Inspector of this-or-that poking his nose into other people's business in the neighbourhood. As an early-warning system it could be profitably adopted by the security-forces of the nation.

You want to join ? Getting onto or into the circuit entails the ability to drink many cups of tea in many farmhouse kitchens. You then show your willingness to co-operate by feeding bits of information into the system. Then after a period of novitiate, you become an accepted member, and you begin to get the hard stuff ... 'the Grape Vine says ...'

Then other occasions. I am not a regular churchgoer, since I live far from a church, and anyway I like my Sunday at home, it being a day when I usually get visitors, but when opportunity offers (i.e. if friends take me) I do go to one or other of the little moorland churches for a service. Having lived in five parishes over the last twenty-odd years I am accepted as a parishioner still in all of them. I love the little grey stone churches, so full of the joys and sorrows and hopes and longing of the farm folk of all the centuries. The simple services where the psalms come alive, fraught with meaning, within this daily world of flocks and herds and corn sown and reaped. 'We are the people of His pasture and the sheep of His hand ... the strength of the hills is His also . . .' The meeting too of friends in the porch as we come out, and more gossip, a chat with the Rector, then home to high-tea. Sunday in the country is a happy casual day to round-off – or rather start – the week.

Another thing which helps to make things tick is the Women's Institute. Most parishes still have their local branches which provide a monthly get-together for the ladies of the community, with interesting talks, a fine tea and of course more gossip!

Of seasonal happenings social wise, Easter is a joyful time marking the end of winter and providing a holiday for visitors, but usually it catches most of us lambing, so counts itself out. I love Easter though, with its proclamation of new life, and always try to get my little home Spring-cleaned and the summer curtains up and daffodils in the vase for Easter Day.

The first big annual event and farmer's holiday – if a farmer can be said to have a holiday this side of autumn – is the County Show. By this of course is meant the Devon County Show at Exeter (West Somerset marches with Devon – it has no affinity with East Somerset). Whoever can go, goes. Such a wonderful day out in a concentrated kaleidoscopic world of fine cattle, sheep, horses, dogs, fur and feather, flowers, crafts, magnificent machinery, military displays and music. So much there is to see and to do, I always come home tired-out, more so than if I had done a day's hard work! After the County Show looms the Bath and West, but few of us get that far, more's the pity, for it's a truly great agricultural show. I am lucky to have been a time or two in my life.

High summer is marked by our Flower Show. This is the Great Day for our village! The Flower show proper in the Hall – flowers, vegetables, cookery, eggs, jams, needlework, knitting, handycrafts, children's painting, etc. – then in the little field by the bridge the fete with teas, sideshows, stalls and children's sports. It is obligatory for everyone to do something. I always show some vegetables and a few flowers. Everybody goes of course, and folk who have left the district come back, and it's a great day for meeting old friends again!

Then the Sheep Dog Trials. A real farmer's day-out this, held on a high wide moorland farm. An afternoon watching the wonderful sagacity of lean collies dealing with wild-eyed bloody-minded hill-sheep. With what pride a winning owner takes home a silver cup!

Next follows the Horse Show, an event drawing both competitors and onlookers from outside the area. A really big event this, specializing in hunters and Exmoor ponies, at which one meets acquaintances from afar and talks 'horse' all day.

Then follow gymkhanas all around, at which you will see the children and the ponies you know competing and enjoying themselves.

Now we're into the Hunting Season. First the Staghounds and then the Foxhounds hold their early meets in August. A meet of the Hounds is always an event to be got to if you can, to see the hounds, to talk to friends, to look at new horses – perhaps a new Master! (The real hunting comes later, later in the day, later in the season, when things have settled down – the best hunting I see is usually round about my own home anyway.)

With September come the first of the sheep and cattle auctions. These are functions of great importance to hill-country folk, for on the bidding can be guaged the strength of the autumn trade. Crowds cram the ways and press around the pens of bleating sheep and bawling cattle, and of course this is a social occasion as well as a business one, to be accompanied like all such with eating, drinking and gossip.

October brings the Harvest Festival, such a joyous occasion, with the Church decorated with flowers, foliage, vegetables and oaten sheaves, and fleeces too (for wool is one of our harvests here) and so full of people that you cannot find a seat if you are late. I love the Harvest Festival with its joyful, almost pagan, offering and thanksgiving for all the fruits and bounty of the earth. Then the Harvest Supper afterwards, in village hall or inn, with feasting and dancing till late into the night. Even the long walk home on a dark stormy night (if I don't get a lift) does not deter me nor keep me away from such festivity.

So the year moves on to Christmas. The great mid-winter festival, part pagan, part Christian, is no-where more well-kept or more rejoiced-in than here in the hill-country. Though beasts must be fed and stock looked-to as usual, no-one does more work about the farm than is necessary over the fortnight that covers Christmas. It's a time of high days and holiday before real winter sets in with the New Year. There's the tying of presents, the decorating of rooms – even I bring in holly and fir to deck my little home and set up the gay cards on my shelves – the baking of cakes, the preparing for parties. There's the Carol Service with the Church all embowered in Christmas greenery and children reading the Lessons. There is Midnight Mass, with the Church windows glowing out into the darkness of another Christmas Eve, and another Christmas Morning when we come home again. There's Christmas dinner with families gathered together, there's the Boxing Day Meet when the quarry most hunted is that out of a bottle and the Boxing Day shoot when it's marvellous if anything's shot. There're parties and dances and whist-drives, and comings and goings all over the place. Oh, what a wonderful time is Christmas! (And if it lasted any longer we'd all be dead of overeating and exhaustion!)

New Year's Eve is the final fling of the festivities (except for those of us who remember Twelfth Night). Now it is the long haul through to the Spring, with the endless rounds of caring for the beasts and battling with the elements of rain, wind, snow and ice.

The cry of the Foxhounds enlivens the short winter days betimes, and happy is he who can find the time and the means to hunt. For me, there are exciting moments whenever hounds are near. Then as winter gives way to Spring, there's the round of Point-to-Points, for a day at the races is tremendous fun. (Five in this region if one can get to them.)

Then there are all the occasional events of the countryside. Farm sales – again great social affairs to which everybody goes who can regardless of intention to buy. Weddings – likewise great affairs, with feasts for wedding-breakfasts, and joy all round. 'Twenty-first' birthday parties – much drinking and dancing – and Christening parties too. So many occasions to fill out a year! . . .

Oh, and I almost forgot what should not be forgotten – the County Library travelling service. Every third Thursday the big rocking van comes down the hill past the head of my track and stops for me to enter the Aladdin's Cave of books, treasure to me as I take first one and then another from the shelves, whole magic worlds between their coloured covers. When I have gathered as many as I can carry in my rucksack and thanked the kindly librarian-driver, I struggle home a mile over the moor, perhaps in the teeth of a raging gale till battered and breathless I plod up my piece of muddy lane, full of the thought of the cosy evening ahead.

And some people say country life is dull – they can never have really tried it!

CHAPTER TWENTY

Paper, Pencil and Brush

FOUR o'clock on a dark November morning, and my hand reaches out to stop the alarm-clock, then I roll out of bed to light the stove and put the kettle on.

A pot of hot tea made and a mug gathered-up, and back to my cosy bunk with said pot of tea in my lap, and then to work. A sheet of blank paper – just that – on a small drawing-board, and a lead-pencil with a chewed and broken end beside it. Here now, to my hand and within my grasp is all of life. Behold, I take up the pencil and write, and here is coherent thought, memory, observation, opinion, proclamation, all inscribed by this simple act with simple materials for as long as these things shall last. Speech is made perhaps immortal. What I write now, if I die tomorrow, will be read by others far into the future. Here is power of a sort.

Of all those things most precious and necessary to me, paper ranks the highest, and being one of those few things which I cannot make for myself, is something for which I have to save up a few pence week by week. However, good paper I use only for important or 'finished' work – split reversed old envelopes, etc., serve for notes and rough sketches.

So much there is to write about. All yesterday's happenings – I keep a journal – thoughts on many things, ideas, records, essays into the past, forward steps into the future. Half-way through I am hungry and get my breakfast. Then I go on until I have done my quota for the day, and stop and arouse myself to the affairs of daylight.

The day moves on. It is afternoon now and the sunshine calls me out to walk and to sketch. I take up my small sketching case and set off. It is one of my precious possessions, this small folding canvas thing that hangs over my shoulder by a sling of webbing. It started life as an army map-case, was given to me, then by me fitted-up for out-door sketching. Unclip its edges and it opens out book-wise and there on one side is paper and hard board in a watertight pocket, on the other a small box of watercolours held by a canvas band, and pencils and paint-brushes beside it likewise held by canvas attachments. An Indian-rubber on a string, a clip-grip for clamping down paper in a wind, and a twelve-bore cartridge case (for holding just enough water for a sketch) corked and pendant on a string likewise, complete the outfit. Observe: everything from paintbox to cork of water-pot is tied-on. Experience has taught me that once you drop something in the undergrowth it is damn difficult to find again and takes up precious time looking for it anyway, so it's better not to lose it in the first place.

So to walk my walk for today. I may be walking to a specific place in the hope of getting a good light on a particular view or I may be just idling along (if ever I do idle!) then be suddenly brought up short by some scene touched by the sun to a breathtaking vision. How shall I describe in words the world in which I walk when I set out to sketch, or the act of sketching itself? As in hunting, every sense is keyed and receptive. Form, colour, depth, movement, time and light enter into one, sounds and scent of things too, and the touch of them, heightening one's awareness of being. Then, suddenly, the play of light upon some natural feature, hill or rock or river, trees gathered in a group, or animals grazing in garland-form, and one feels communion with these and with Something for which there is no word. Then the urge to reach for paper and colours and to make some deeper, personal contact with it. To try to reach out and hold in some way this fleeting moment of marvel and make it immortal – but that is vain, vanity on the part of the artist, because no hand can ever truly touch the reality. Yet something commands. So to sit down, amongst wet foliage as like as not, or crouched uncomfortably on hard ground. Out with paint box, etc., to make the attempt. How futile it is, to try and match all this compound wonder of shape and colour, light and shadow, this unmatchable marvel of Creation! Yet one tries, and as one works, however poorly, draws close to things beyond conscious understanding. The hand traces and tries to match curve and contour, tree and stone, soaring cloud and running water, though the mind realizes its own inadequacy. Yet the eye sees with both outer and inner intensity as never before. Once a friend said to me, 'You never really see a thing until you draw it'. How great a truth – until you sit down before a place or a thing and really look at it in the way an artist must in order to translate it to his own two-dimensional rendering, you have never truly seen it. Now you perceive the true marvel of all shapes and forms, from the branches of trees on the skyline to the frond of bracken by your side, from the outspread wings of a bird to the folds of wool on the neck of a sheep, all textures from those of rough stone to the smooth hide of a horse.

Then, transcendent splendour, colour. Colour is one of the great emotional forces of life. Its richness, its stimulation, its satisfaction of the eye is a sensual pleasure. It inspires a delight comparable to eating and drinking, enhancing the more mystical wonder of form. The blue of the sky, the green of grass, the myriad colours of summer flowers, the furnace-colours of autumn, the subtle greys and browns of winters. The light playing with the colours, running with them, transposing them into harmonies like great music. Even so, how shall one make any likeness of this? Yet one tries.

As to the plain and practical work, my little paintbox carries just eight colours, each the brightest of its sort. (You can always soften-down colours – you cannot make them stronger or clearer – so I choose the brightest.) Two blues, a violet-tinged blue (cobalt or ultramarine) and a cold blue (cerulean). Two yellows, a cold yellow (lemon cadmium) and a warm golden-yellow (cadmium). Two reds, a flame-red (vermilion) and a crimson-red (alizarin). A rich russet as a basis for browns (burnt-sienna) and a dense black (lamp). With these eight colours you can get all the colours in creation that it is possible to get with pigments. They are enough. If you have more, you only get confused. With only these few, each occupying its own place in the paintbox, you get to know them almost blindfold, and can reach for them almost without taking your eyes off the scene before you (which is, when quickness is essential in sketching rapidly-moving light and colour, a real help). Also, you learn to mix colours to get exact effects, which is an art in itself – if you have too many colours you tend to use them 'raw' and not to reach for the subtleties that mirror Nature. (Yes, well, I admit I cheat from this order sometimes, when the greens of Spring and autumn are very strong, and I then carry an extra colour – viridian. A very dangerous colour for a would-be landscape painter, I know, but I can't resist its gorgeous brilliance just for a touch here and there.)

The paper held by my small case is just the right size for out-door sketching, about 10" x 7". Smaller than this, and the work is cramped, larger and the paper flaps about in the wind. Of brushes I have two, a middling-sized one for general work and a small sable for any precision needed.

Myself, I tend to work in a way not generally advocated in the handling of watercolour – 'dry', using the colour in strokes as far as possible, and avoiding sloppy wet 'washes'. I find it easier to control things under outdoor conditions if I don't get my paper too wet. Also, it makes possible the use of cheaper paper than is otherwise necessary.

As I work, the scene before me becomes part of me and I of it and I forget all else. Then having at length done as much as I feel able to do, I rise and find how cramped I am, and probably cold and wet as well! For, let me say, sketching is not an affair of sunny days only, but of stormy ones too. It is often in times of wild wind, with great black clouds bursting in squalls and with sudden shafts of scalding sunshine streaming from the rifts that the most dramatic scenes are presented to one. In times of snow too, when trees stand in black patterns out of the void of white, or bitter east winds clear the sky to a cold brittle blue above drifts that are rose and violet before the low winter sun. Often I've worked until the water freezing on brush and palette made further attempts impossible. The true outdoor artist needs to have the dedication and toughness of a wildfowler!

When I get home I spread my small sketches out and date and annotate them, prior to filing them away for future use. (If and when I need any of them for book illustrations they must be either carefully finished off or entirely redrawn according to process.) Small and inadequate though these sketches are, somehow I feel I have in some way brought home a fragment out of life and time and hold it in my hands. Each little picture proclaims that here was a moment in a place and I was there – and still am. In some way I have captured, and hold, a treasure out of the heart of Creation. So must ancient Man have felt when he, with pigments of fat and oxide, drew the beasts of his world upon the walls of caves. To him was known the truth of magic that when your hand has drawn a thing, you have power over it, in some way hold and possess it.

The first artist of the world was a magician and the magician was an artist. Perhaps it is still so.

CHAPTER TWENTY ONE

Storm

S OMEONE once said to me, this is a country where you feel the full
force of Nature. How true this is, I have found over the years.
Living as I do, I have to meet all the elements head-on and cope
with them how I can, and in so doing have learned much.

Something folk nurtured in urban surroundings and insulated against
the rawness of natural life fail to estimate is the sheer overwhelming
power of Nature. For most of them, it seems, the elemental forces of
rain, snow, fire, wind and the sea, are just the things that are either
pretty or a nuisance as the case may be and not to be heeded more than
that. Consequently there are scores, perhaps hundreds of cases of
foolhardy people in trouble with the elements – most especially with the
sea – every year.

I myself, from childhood on a wild Atlantic coast onwards to years in
western hill-country, have learned something of Nature's power. How
also to meet it and deal with it as far as is humanely possible, whilst

respecting it greatly. I would not survive in my present way of life if I did not.

Storm is part of life in this country where the fierce Atlantic gales sweep in from the ocean to flay the high ground and pour torrents of rain on the watershed. Iron in the hills draws fearful lightning and in the winter snow at this altitude (over 1,000 ft.) becomes a raging blizzard burying everything. Fire too is a hazard when the moor has been parched by sun and drying winds.

The years have taught me to make due assessment of the weather. Of these violent forces, strong wind may be said to be the most prevalent. Rarely are there completely calm days and at any time of year a fresh breeze may mount up to a howling gale in next-to-no-time. Such a gale will rip off roofs, tear off rick-sheets and half the rick as well, tumble hen houses and bring down trees and even knock a Land-Rover off the road without the slightest hesitation. It will bowl you over too if you suddenly meet it on an exposed corner. It behoves the dweller in the hills to see his roofs are sound and strong and roped down where necessary. With roofs proper the damage is usually done by the wind getting its fingers in under the eaves or into a weak place in the roof itself and so wrenching it off like a box-lid. (As a child I remember slate roofs being 'grouted' with cement on the seaward side to prevent this, whilst ricks were laced-over with ropes weighted down with huge stones to stop them 'taking-off'.) Where you have anything roped down you must frequently examine the ropes for fretting and fraying (the incessant rain helps to rot them very quickly) and replace where necessary while the weather is fine – or you will find your defences tearing to pieces in a pounding gale and have to go out and wrestle with the elements to save the situation. Of this and the hazards of flying slates and falling branches, I think I have already spoken.

The usual complement to high wind is streaming driving rain. With all the mighty fetch of the Atlantic behind it the rain here can come down as though it meant to float you away like Noah. Again your roofs must be sound and your walls too, for backed by a remorseless Souwester it will blow in anywhere. Though continuous thick driving drizzle tends to be the usual form of precipitation hereabouts, violent cloud-burst type of storms are not infrequent on the highest hills, and therein lies a danger to valley-dwellers. Sudden heavy rain on the watershed of the high moor will cause all the streams that flow therefrom to rise with great rapidity and become boiling coffee-coloured torrents, which, discharging their headwater into already-full rivers will quickly flood the lower valleys. Don't live in a valley if you can help it, and never camp on a river-bank! Just one hour's deluge on the hilltops miles upstream can wash you out without warning. (The dreadful Lynmouth flood-disaster of '52 was an extreme example of this – mercifully, such a catastrophy occurs but rarely in history, nevertheless, minor similarities happen somewhere or other most years.)

If, outward bound, your way lies across a ford and the stream is already full and rising, with dark storm-clouds up the valley, think twice before you cross that stream. You may return to find your little ford a maelstrom of rushing whirling brown water, impossible to recross – and a night in a wet valley waiting for the water to go down isn't funny. Needless to say, never plunge into a river running in spate, even if you don't think it is very deep – it is always deeper than you think, and the force with which hill-streams run when they are full and angry has to be experienced to be believed – it is better to believe and not experience – and they will drown unwary sheep without hesitation and even sweep away a man on horseback. Significantly, the Devon and Somerset Staghounds usually cancel meets in deep-valley areas when the rivers are in full spate – the fords are then considered too deep and dangerous for both hounds and horses.

Another way in which torrential rain vents its feelings on the land is in the gouging of gullies and the tearing-out of road surfaces. You may have quite a good hard-core farm road one day and one that looks like the craters of the moon the next. Coming home in the dark after a violent storm, it is as well to test the ground before you – if the genie of the storm has been at work on your road, there may be rents and gullies in it enough to fall head-first into – I once pitched full-length into a gully that was full of black peat-ooze and I could never get the stains out of my clothing no matter how hard I washed them!

Thunderstorms crash savagely around the hills from time to time, the lightning stabbing viciously at the iron lodes deep within the rocks. The lurid flashes illuminate the night and set one's nerves a-tingling, whilst the ground vibrates as the thunder-rolls go echoing down the valleys. Seldom is there no damage by the morning – most storms bring an aftermath of struck trees and fences, with cattle and sheep dead underneath. A violent thunderstorm is no time to be abroad if you can avoid it. Stay in your own home if you can.

At the other extreme, one of the specialities of this country is hill-mist, the thick white fog, that can descend on the highground at any time without warning, blotting out everything and muffling you as though in a strange white tent. Sometimes it is so thick and opaque that you cannot see more than a yard or so around you. To move away from a known track or fence is to risk being hopelessly lost, for the hill-mist, unlike the blackness of night, has the peculiar effect of deadening all sense of direction. You walk in a curious halfworld, one of unformed life, like the void before Creation, with such objects as are visible at all strangely unreal and uncertain in distance. Once such white fog has set in, there is no telling when it may lift – maybe in a few hours, maybe not for a week or more.

More often than not, the usual accompaniment to the fog is drizzle. Just fine drizzle, the 'misty wet' of the hills, making everything wet and dripping and relentlessly turning the earth to squelching splashing mud. Such weather is not usually cold, rather the reverse, and it is now that humidity brings forth moulds and fungi. Even indoors everything tends to be clammy and anything wet and not dried-out at once develops a black mould, which, in the case of textiles won't wash out. One just puts up with it – it's all that one can do, as with the rest of the weather!

Winter brings frost and ice, and snow, though not usually until after Christmas. Front when it comes sets the ground like concrete and all waters save the fast-running streams turn to ice. Since I do not like a stuffy bedroom and always sleep with the window open, letting the stove out when I go to bed, the temperature of the interior of my tiny little home drops by dawn to that of the outer air, and commonly when I wake-up everything that can freeze is frozen stiff: the water bucket almost solid ice, the lids of kettle and tea-pot frozen-on, eggs (if I've got any) split with the cold, and, if I have not remembered to drain my flower-jug before turning-in, that will be split too (I've lost several favourite vases that way) whilst often the hoar-frost sparkles on the walls and ceiling. However, a quickly-made fire and a boiling kettle soon warm things up. The simplest way of unfreezing the water in the bucket is to heat the flat-iron and stand on the ice! (Some folk shudder at the thought of such an awakening, but I am myself convinced that this Spartan living is one of the reasons I never have coughs, colds or other ills.) And once out of doors, it's dry and usually gloriously sunny as the morning advances!

Snow is something no one looks forward to in these parts, for when it comes it is usually in the form of fierce blizzards, and this is sheep-country and sheep are most vulnerable in heavy snow. As to what snow can be like in this country, well, I have many memories of many blizzards. Snow whirling like blind white smoke, snow driving in horizontal sheets, thick as a wall, on a wind so bitter that neither sheep nor cattle will face it, drifts mounting high as gateways, high as hedges, high as roofs. Lanes filled-in to the tops of their banks, sheep buried, tractors buried, snow-ploughs buried. Telegraph poles snapped-off at their roots and flung across the moor in a welter of wires. Days of desperate digging, digging out sheep, digging out gateways, digging out doorways. Days of struggle to feed the beasts, days of being cut-off from the rest of the world. Days followed by nights so bitter that the dung freezes to the shippon floor as it drops. Every farm so cut-off must fend for itself and look to its own needs without hope of outside help. Wise folk will have good stores of food-stuffs for man and beast and a good wood-pile in the yard before the onset of winter, and come to no harm. Myself, I always lay-in 'iron rations' sufficient for four months, just before Christmas (not that one expects snow to last that long – but it did in '63).

The hazards of snow are many, from getting lost in a blinding blizzard, being smothered in fresh drifts, collapsing from exhaustion on open ground, to being chopped by a mass of snow suddenly descending from shippon roofs as it thaws. (The *weight* of packed snow is something you believe when you have been hit by some of it.) No-one but a fool goes beyond the shelter of hedge-banks in a blizzard, nor out at all except to see to the safety of beasts. Some there are who have died because of foolhardiness.

Something too, not always realized, is that snow drifts on the lee side of hedges and walls – that is why sheep bury, seeking shelter from the blast.

One thing, though, one can never be short of in deep snow, is water! It has come as a great surprise to me to hear folk say sometimes they have been in sore straights for water because their plumbing has frozen-up. Well, one bucket full of snow renders down to a third of water very quickly, so you can't really die of thirst!

A terrible elemental force, perhaps the most frightening of all, is fire. In this moorland country 'swaling' or late-winter burning-off of old over-grown heather and gorse is part of heath-management, but unfortunately this is not always undertaken with as much care as it should be. In a high March wind a heath-fire will be out of control in next-to-no-time. Worse still, in a hot dry summer stupid holiday-makers will start fires in dry scrub in all sorts of ways from lighting camp-fires and dropping cigarette-butts to leaving glass bottles about to act as burning-glasses. A summer bush-fire is worse than a Spring one, because the ground beneath the scrub is parched dry and the very earth will burn. The sight of heavy smoke, undershot with the lurid glow of flames, coming your way, is a terrifying thing. But it is no good being frightened. You have to *do* something about it. There is only one way to tackle a bush-fire – to beat it back.

Twice I have had to tackle a heath-fire single-handed. Once when some idiot got the marsh below on fire, once when a swaling-fire jumped the boundary-hedge on the hill and started to eat its way towards my homestead. I cut green branches for a broom, dipped them in water (and splashed some water over myself) and then went to meet the fire.

You must beat and trample, beat the fire back on itself, trample the smouldering ground, working up and down the line of advance, looking every now and then over your shoulder to see if a wind-driven spark has leapt on to start a fresh fire behind you – if it has, you must go back and get it out at once, then return to the main line of fire. When at last – God willing – you have got the fire under control, it will soon go out for lack of fuel, but still you must patrol up and down for hours, because sparks may smoulder for many hours in the hot peaty soil to fan into another outbreak if you leave too soon.

Thus twice I have got fires out that were burning on fronts of sevel hundred yards. I got blackened and scorched, and once almost collapsed with exhaustion, but I prevailed – Amen!

Oh, if only some folk would have a little care for their actions, a little imagination for the consequences before they start a fire!

H.L.B.

CHAPTER TWENTY TWO

Kingdom of Dreams

WERE I asked what is the greatest treasure of life, the deepest wonder of being, I would answer, imagination.

It is the wondrous thing, the alchemy of the mind, the true magic of the human head and heart. The essence of the life-force, all power lies within it. Desire a thing, and imagination both conjures up its fulfilment and opens doors to its accomplishment.

The gift of imagination is the spark of godhead within the individual, and godlike are its powers. Given as a birthright to every child, it illuminates the world of youth, then, sadly so often seems to flicker out as age advances. That is, for most people. Some there are though, who keep it all their lives, and they are rich beyond the dreams of avarice did they but know it.

For me, imagination has been a life-long companion. Stepping into the wonder of life as a child, imagination enhanced everything. Toys came to life, fairies peeped from around the garden-plants, ogres lurked in the dark corners of the night, dreams of delight followed the sunbeams down the meadows. I held long conversations with everything, and wove stories about every object that came my way.

Then came practical use. Imagination showed me how to obtain something I wanted, to make things, to achieve some difficult task, to turn thoughts and feelings into pictures that conveyed a meaning.

Finally, imagination took me on wings out into time and space, into the boundlessness of all that has been, and is, and may be, and gave me dreams of power and how things could be.

Imagination has remained with me all my life, a force mightier than anything else, one which can touch the commonplace into such a wonder that the mind can scarcely contain it, that can conjure great dreams and endow one's consciousness with a thousand lives. It has sustained me in times of frustration and great disappointment, encouraged me to make new ventures, and illuminated pathways into the future. Imagination is life, lack of it, death before its time.

So, at every point and turn imagination goes with me. I walk around the garden, and leaves and stems and flowers weave themselves into wonderful and exotic designs through which I see the faces of satyrs. I look around my little home and I see a thread-bare bed-cover and think how nice something gay and fresh would look, only I haven't enough money to buy a new one. Imagination suggests rainbow patchwork (I've lots of odd pretty bits of stuff stored away) with cushion-covers to match – then it really gets going and I see visions of beautiful covers all made of fragments of jewel-like colour worked into intricate patterns of flower and animal forms. Then my little bantam cock passes the open door (the little devil will be inside in a moment if I don't stop him, and up to heaven-knows-what wickedness) and I see rich drapings with gorgeous cock-patterns on them, splendid as Byzantine brocades. I start to work out a fairly simple practical means of making such – then have to face the fact that there just isn't enough time in my life for this, and any patchwork will have to be of the simplest sort.

I see a pair of old rather dilapidated but fine-formed goat's horns in the back of my general-purpose shed (they are on a skull-top – a trophy given to me many years ago). Imagination says, a Pan head! Get clay or papier-mache and model a mocking satyr's face, bearded and long-eared, onto the skull, paint it nut-brown and gild the horns – what a magnificent wall-ornament! But alas, common-sense says, even if I spent the time on it, I haven't the wall-space on which to hang it. Old legs of Victorian furniture chucked out on a wood-pile suggest the pillars of sundial and birdbath – and I actually have made a sundial out of one such piece.

Whenever I see a house being built or an old one being renovated, at once my imagination gets to work, and I visualize what I would have made of it – of course something quite different from what present owners are doing with it. I plot and plan everything from shape and size to the finishing paints and textures, right down to things like ornamental weather-vanes and creepers up the walls! In the end I guess I get as much fun out of it as the owners who will live in it – and I don't have to pay for it!

As I walk about the country, seeing fine views and coming to sheltered spots, imagination goes with me and says ever and anon, 'now what would it be like to live just here?' At once I see the sort of dwelling that would fit this very place, how it should be orientated and how it should look and where the approach should be, and feel what it would be like to wake up in the morning here. And a garden! Yes, I can see all the possibilities – the terraces, the stream turned into waterfalls, the natural rock garden, the bog full of exotic plants, the view framed by trees. Such a lovely dream!

Then the landscape itself. If I owned all of it, how I would mould it with woods and plantations, grouped to enhance a view, set to give shelter to stock, making a contrast and a balance to fine sweeps of moorland or green fields. How this bit of land would make better pasture, how that odd bit could be left to go wild. What animals I would introduce. How a proper balance between wild and tame, agriculture and beauty, might be made.

From this, my thoughts will go on to society itself, asking myself why things are as bad as they are and how they could be made better. Imaginings of a better state of things, with a different scale of values, saner government and juster laws, and how such could be achieved, run through my mind.

Then comes night-time, and out of the night more dreams as I sit before my fire or lie cosy in my bed. Boundless dreams out of time and space. I see the whole round world, and coached by books go travelling in every place. On the wings of imagination I step backwards and forwards in time, seeing the land that is around me as it was in the beginning when men first saw it, all scrub and thicket and marsh, with strange wild beasts the denizens of its wilderness, and Nature supreme. I see it as it might be again, its primal hills and valleys outlasting the feet of modern man.

Even beyond the realms of Earth something within me goes. Out into unlimitable space, reaching out for New Worlds somewhere amongst the stars. I seem to see and to walk amongst landscapes never seen on Earth, with trees and flowers unknown to earthly eyes, and beasts fantastical never created here.

I long to draw and write of the things I see in dreams, but there is never enough time for even a fragment of this. Oh why is life so short, that a thousand lives could not live what is in one small human mind and brain? Why, in one human head are there unnumbered kingdoms, worlds, universes, yet only three-score-and-ten years to experience or accomplish the tiniest fragment of what is therein? Why such colossal imbalance and waste? Yet perhaps all this may be a perception of Life as it *Is*, of which this immediate earthly life is but a day among all the days and nights that follow each other in the endless stream of eternity?

What is imagination? Much may the biologists and psychologists talk and analyse, but in the end they do not know. Like all the great mysteries of being it is unfathomable. It can only be experienced, felt, and used. It is the most enormous power there is. It opens doors of perception far beyond those of material understanding. Good and Evil dwell within it - take care with such a power, for there are principalities of terror as well as realms of joy within it.

It governs all things. As you think, feel and imagine, so you will act. If I think, out of my imagination that someone or something is going to do me good, then I am full of pleasure and anticipation. If I think something is going to harm me, then I am aggressive and apprehensive, with accompanying physical sensations. The stark fact that neither may be so, or happen, has nothing to do with the reality of the reactions and sensations.

Yet in all things imagination is the vital spark. Some folk dismiss dreams and dreamers as impractical, but this is unjust and untrue. Imagination is a most practical and necessary thing. Without imagination there can be no forward-looking, no foreseeing of anything. 'Where there is no vision the people perish.'

The General on the battlefield must have the imagination to foresee both the possible moves of his enemy and the probable results of his own manoeuvres. The Statesman must have the vision to foresee the consequences of his acts in the affairs of government. The driver of a heavy vehicle needs sufficient imagination to visualize an accident if certain things happen in conjunction. Half the horrors of life happen because the people who commit or precipitate them have no imagination. Ecological destruction, wars, human tragedies, heartbreak, the hurt feelings of a child – all can be traced to sheer lack of imagination. From the simplest things of daily life to the soaring per-ceptions of the poet and mystic, imagination is the spark that ignites fire. Perhaps it is well that we do not know too much about it. Perhaps it is too great, too elemental a thing to use as we have used the atom. It is unlimitable power that sits in the kingdom of the mind. It is the daemon within.

And sometimes people say to me, 'Aren't you ever *bored*?'

CHAPTER TWENTY THREE

Thoughts

IN MY daily life there is ample scope for thoughts and thinking. Walking on the hills, going about my chores, pausing between bouts of reading and writing, eating my supper, sitting by the fire on a winter's evening, settling down in bed at night, I think a lot and about all sorts of things.

First of course come the thoughts of what I must do about this and that, and such matters as concern my daily life and well-being. Then, beyond these, sometimes arising from them, or from something observed in the world around me, or perhaps triggered-off by something heard on the radio, come other more abstract thoughts. The mind considers, questions. Sometimes it draws conclusions, more often it halts at the alpha and omega of all askings: Why?

Now wandering thoughts may by some be dismissed as idle, yet to my mind they are important. They mould attitudes to religion, politics and society in general. They are the prelude to an outlook on life and to any future action. So I think, I question, sometimes I conclude, but mostly I just *think*.

The subject I find myself most frequently dwelling upon is that of relative values. It is something which concerns myself and my way of life directly, then extends to the land around me and afar to the towns and cities that I occasionally (though very rarely) visit. Here all around me is a countryside that is beautiful and fruitful, still with a balance between wild beauty, comfortable farms and pleasant villages. Here is good neighbourliness, friendship, satisfaction. By and large health and happiness too. Practical matters, work, sport and pleasure go hand in hand. The whole comprises what I regard as a balanced life.

Sometimes though I see for a few hours another sort of life, as when I get the occasional lift into town to buy a few things that I cannot get in the village.

At first, for a couple of hours, I enjoy charging round the shops, buying what I can afford, gloating over what I can't, lingering to 'window shop'. Then the grimness of it all overwhelms me. The snarling traffic making it fearful to cross the streets, the ceaseless noise, the foul smell of fume-laden air, the garish lights, the drabness behind the glitter, the deadness of concrete and tarmac underfoot, the soul-lessness of the towering walls of brick and concrete shutting out the sunlight. People crowd the pavements, they are all well-dressed, they all carry expensive purchases on their arms, they dive in and out of expensive shops, but their faces are pale, they do not smile, they seem worried and preoccupied, no one stops to talk, they all seem in a hurry. The Affluent Society – may I be forgiven for saying thank God I don't belong to it. Then at last, the journey home. Oh, how thankful I am as the car turns away from the main streets and heads for the country again. (By this time I have a headache and feel knocked-flat.) But how long it takes to leave the urban area. Even when the commercial centre drops behind, suburbia continues for perhaps many miles and every year I notice how the tentacles reach further and further into the countryside, eating up the green fields and farms. More brick and concrete, more noise and foul air, more crowded and dissatisfied humanity, less fertile earth to produce food, less beauty to rest the eye upon, less space and freedom and fresh air. Where will it end?

Why has mankind elected to live in cities? Because, say the knowledgeable ones, we must have industry and culture, because men must have jobs. True enough up to a point, I do not dispute it. But why must towns be forever growing, larger and larger, growing into cities, consuming the countryside like a cancer?

Why cannot towns remain pleasantly small, with fields and woods within walking distance? Why cannot more people live and work in friendly villages and on the land as I am sure Nature intended them to?

Population and economics says the oracle. With the first I will not wholly disagree. A sudden mass exodus would indeed swamp the countryside. Nevertheless, many more thousands, perhaps millions, *could* live a rural life without disturbance of the present-day countryside in any way, were the social-economic climate a little different. How? I look around and I see half the dwellings in almost every parish around here, from small cottages to large farmhouses, turned into holiday-cottages, occupied only for a few months, perhaps only weeks, in the year. Looking deeper, I see ruins of small homesteads all about, their walls masked by brambles, or half-forgotten in some combe. I see that most of the farms today consist of an amalgamation of two or more smaller farms. The countryside is in fact being depopulated.

Then work, says the economist. People cannot get jobs in the country of a sort to maintain a 'standard of living'. Why not, and what is a 'standard of living'? One acre of land will provide a family with all the food they can eat in terms of vegetables and fruit and a little meat. (An acre of ground well-cultivated will produce at least ten tons of fresh food – enough for a family of five, with something left over for feeding to small livestock for meat.) Five acres will support grain and a dairy-beast. For the further needs of life, why should not the smallholder pursue a craft, trade or profession in his own home or in a local centre? Let every sort of home-craft and village-industry be encouraged. And what is wrong with establishing light industry proper in the larger villages and small townships? The small neat factory is no more unsightly than the large modern concrete-and-composition agricultural building.

Oh, says the economist, such a community could not pay the taxes to support the Welfare State. Well, why should it? If people lived healthier, happier and more self-reliant lives they would not need the blanket-smother of the 'social services'.

Maybe such a society and economy would not be able to afford the endless spate of mass-produced use-once-and-throw-away goods that now proliferate everywhere. But why should this be the criterion of a prosperous society? We all have too much and waste too much nowadays. Is it not better to have fewer material goods and to live in a world of natural bounty, with the fruits of a fertile earth to eat, fresh air to breathe, and a lovely landscape to rest one's eyes upon? Is it not better to do without superfluous luxuries and live in good fellowship with one's neighbours, without crime or the fear of crime as folk of the hill-country do? Is it not better to creatively make things for oneself than to be slavishly dependent on mass-produced products? Is it not better to be one's own master in some personal endeavour than to be slavishly bound to something or someone you hate?

The chief stumbling-block to any such rural resettlement is of course the bone-headedness of the Powers-that-Be. Which leads one to thoughts of Government. It has been said that the mentality of a mob is that of its lowest member, and this goes for governmental bodies in general. Whether local or national, they are characterized by their almost total lack of imagination or appreciation of anything other than or beyond immediate materialism, or of any need other than to catch votes by pandering to whatever is in current favour.

All Governments are bad, but some are worse than others. With this statement, some time made by some wise man, I wholeheartedly agree, and to it I add, whichever one is in power at the moment is the worst because it is the one you have to put up with. Of the varied forms of government, that called Local Government is the worst of all. It can only be likened to a vicious mule with kicking hindquarters at one end and no brain at the other.

A peculiar manifestation of Local Government is its Fascist-like tyranny over the lives of citizens, dictating to them whether they shall have homes or not, what sort of homes they may or may not have, and what they may or may not do within those homes and whether or not they may earn a living at all.

The strangulation of freedom augmented by crushing taxation seems to be the main function of all statutory bodies. Taxation at its present level and in its innumerable forms is iniquitous. When it reaches, collectively, more than half the income of the average citizen (as recent statistics say that it does) it becomes legalized robbery, and immoral. One of the worst impositions of all upon the individual is the exorbitant locally-levied tax called Rates, crushing and often cruel in its extraction. It is a tax on living, on the home which is the right of every man, like a tax on a bird's nest or a rabbit's bunny-hole.

What is Freedom? Freedom is the right to live and do as you wish, so long as you do no harm to your neighbour. Freedom is the right to be in a job and belong to Trades Union, or to work for yourself in your own backyard and belong to no Union. It is the right of persons to have luxuries in their home and to pay for them, or the right not to have them, and not to pay for them.

Well, I suppose we must have some laws and some taxation in order to maintain a State at all and to prevent anarchy. Fair enough – but let the power of Government, fiscal and otherwise, be kept to the necessary minimum.

Carried to extremes – which is anything beyond the said minimum – taxation becomes of itself immoral – when an overall exorbitant rate is levied and more and more folk are mulct of more and more of their money to subsidize things they don't want, don't need and may even disapprove of, to the end that the frugal support the wasteful and the sensible are subject to the stupid, whilst all the time beaurocracy proliferates like mushroom spawn and innane rules and regulations receive the status of law to cripple anyone who tries to practise common-sense, then the bounds of righteousness have long been passed. I say, let people keep their own money and spend it as they will, by themselves, or in free association with others.

Independence becomes harder and harder as life becomes entangled in the complexity of rates, taxes, insurances, mortgages, hire-purchase and all the petty laws that go with the lot. The average person of today is as one enmeshed in the dreadful net of the *retiarius* of the Roman arena, unable to break from its deadly cords. Few have the strength to rend its toils.

What about the Social Services, folk say. So we're back to them again. Well, what about them? Apart from a Health Service which I agree is just (for illness or accident come to most sooner or later), it is my opinion that cradle-to-the-grave blanket-cover Social Security is the undoing of the Nation. It atrophies the qualities of free will, self-help, initiative and personal pride.

What about education, they also say. Well, I am of the opinion that children who have no aptitude for any positive career are better out of school and doing something useful. And there's always plenty that wants doing all around – there's never enough labour on the land or help in the home nor hands to do odd jobs anywhere in town or country. And it wouldn't hurt the kids to have more exercise (i.e. work and walk) and less smart clothes and sweets.

I guess I could go on saying a lot more in like vein, but this chapter would be over-full if I did. In the end, laudable though the idea that the strong should help the weak and the fortunate the unfortunate may be in the abstract, in real life it doesn't work out like that. In practice the Welfare State subsidizes the feckless, the irresponsible and the downright lazy at the expense of the self-reliant, the enterprising and the hard-working.

Of life and society in general, the greatest lack of the present day for most people is that of any sort of challenge or adventure. Everything, from what is left of our few square miles of wilderness-land to personal opportunity is, or is in the process of being, so tamed-down that there is little of anything remaining to satisfy the deeper, more fundamental instincts.

Hereabouts, in this region which is now a National Park, I see the process at work – car-parks and mod. cons., all about the moor, tracks turned to tarmac roads, signs everywhere, waymarked paths penetrating into the heart of it. Everything possible is being done to make everything easy, to take away the slightest element of risk. So in the end the concept of conserving the wilderness is defeated by the conservers and made a mockery. For truly wild land is untamed land, hard, ruthless and full of danger. This is its nature, it cannot be otherwise, and herein lies its power and its virtues. It offers challenge, adventure, calls for strenuous physical effort, self-reliance and the taking of risks. Tame it down, make it safe and easy for all comers, and you destroy both its nature and its benefit to humanity.

Deep in the heart and being of Man there is the need, I am convinced, for these things: challenge, danger, adventure, achievement. All of which are being steadily eliminated from modern life. Some people, I know, shrink in their conscious minds from the elements of risk and danger. Yet this is the paradox of life, that life is only to be experienced in full and at its most intense on the edge of danger. Unless you risk a crash and a fall you do not experience the exhilaration of racing or hunting, unless you pit yourself against the elements, you do not know the triumph of climbing a mountain or crossing a wilderness or sailing the sea. Without risk, whether in physical living or in a business venture, there is no excitement and no true satisfaction. Take away all danger and all initiative and life becomes a dull grey, like a paintbox whose bright colours have all been mixed and dulled-down to a colourless mess. The brighter the sun the darker the shadows, the darker the shadows the brighter the light. It is ever so.

These thoughts lead on to others concerning health and energy. Despite the boasts of modern medicine, the majority of people seem far from healthy and even further from fitness, they tire easily, have little energy or drive, and not much real zest for life. I am often surprised, when out walking, at seeing people much younger than myself labouring up hills, awkward in scrambling over rocks or in negotiating rough places, unable to run and jump. Then, amongst my contemporaries, a tendency to strokes, heart-failure, and all sorts of other ills. That which is to blame, I am sure, is the effeteness of modern life, which does its best to obviate the need for effort, physical and otherwise, from childhood onwards. Again, I am convinced that many of the ills of today are due to lack of vigorous bodily exercise. Modern Man is an overfed under-exercised animal. No one can be truly healthy who does not take proper exercise at all stages of life.

Another trend in modern life is that towards excessive specialization. Now I know that one person cannot know or do *everything* in a diverse and complex world, and that some degree of specialization is therefore necessary, but carried to extremes it is a thoroughly bad thing. The classic definition of a specialist as someone who knows more and more about less and less is only too true. The person who is geared to only one job or profession in life, knowing little or nothing about anything else, will have an unbalanced outlook on life, and be at a loss to turn his hand to anything else when the need arises. Even to the man who must follow a specialist career, I would recommend that he find time to do something in life that is the antithesis of his main work, so as to balance himself (the scientist should study art, the artist agriculture, etc.) Nor should he neglect the simple fundamental things of life, such as self-help in home life or in time of emergency. Over-specialization is dangerous. Man has survived as a species largely because he has been unspecialized and omnivorous. Remember the dinosaurs!

So many more things I could go on saying and asking, but this over-long chapter must be brought to an end. What shall I say to conclude it?

I have just been listening to the eight-o'clock news, full as usual of economic troubles and suggestions for the remedying. As always the panacea for all ills is industry, more industry, bigger industry, industry on a more massive scale. Industry must always come first, they say.

To me it is the road to Hell. If I were someone in power, I would say, put the land first. Conservation, agriculture, forestry, a good and healthy rural economy, then industry to match this. History holds a moral, for all great civilizations arose upon a flourishing agriculture and declined upon a failing one. Destroy the cities, and the land will still live and raise civilization again. Destroy the countryside and all will die.

CHAPTER TWENTY FOUR

The Joy of Days

FOR ME, the joy of life is the joy of days, beginning anew each morning, for in a place such as this every day is an adventure. How lovely are the days of life when one lives them to the full! How wonderful, how marvellous, are the simplest things of life, how great a miracle the commonplace! Who could ever weary of the adventure of the days?

Dawn and sunrise, the brightness of midday, sunset and dusk. The sweet days of Spring, the long full days of summer, the fiery days of autumn, the cold short precious ones of winter. Sunshine and rain, wind, frost and snow. Every day, every hour, every moment of every day, its own self and no other, vibrant with life and fraught with decision and drama. Each day a link in the chain of days, stretching from the hidden past into the unguessed future, each my own, my very own in the matrix of being.

Who would waste so precious a thing as a day, an hour, or even a single minute? Waste money, or goods, if you will, but never waste Time. How shall one not waste time? Not indeed by hurrying and scurrying, but by doing just those things worthwhile, by looking and listening, by perceiving all the incredible glory that is encompassed in one day, and giving thanks for such gifts of God.

For myself, I rise early. To do otherwise is to miss half the day, for the first hours are vital and you can never make up for time lost. (I can never understand people who lie abed while the sun is up, wasting the precious hours in meaningless sleep – they lose half their lives – I can only conclude that their lives mean so little to them so that they are half-dead inside themselves already.) I like to be up before sunrise all the year round, and in the winter before dawn, to be ahead of the day, to salute each new morning of life as it comes. For each day is one that has never been yet, nor ever will be again, and you must do honour to it, so that when one lies down again at night one can give thanks to God for all the wonderful things beheld and for work well done and something worthwhile accomplished.

I write now at the dawn of a November day. The small lamp at my shoulder gives light to my paper, but all the while my eyes lift to the window on the other side, the east window above my bunk through which I watch the coming of a new morning. The sky in the east grows pale, and I can just see the dark line of the hills below it. Soon it will glow golden, or be flushed with rose or crimson. Then a moment of intense waiting, with the trees black silhouettes against the light. Then behold, bursting in sudden glory over the rim of the world, the sun! Hail God of the Morning, Eye of the Day, Lord of Life! For a few minutes I am a sun-worshipper, one with all the untold millions since the beginning of time, whilst the golden light floods out over the land, gilding the hilltops with its splendour, chasing the blue shadows out of the combes and warming the cold earth with its growing power.

Another dawn, another day, in which to do so much and when I lie down tonight there will be another one, tomorrow. Not all sunrises will be brilliant, not all days will be fair, but the fullness of a day with all its challenge and manifold delights will be there.

So the promise of the days lies before me. Winter is ahead now, its days short and cold and its night long. Christmas will come soon, with all its hustle and bustle of getting letters and cards off to friends, then all its jollity of parties and feasting. Then the days of winter proper (for in this hill-country real winter begins after Christmas and it is Candlemass Day – February 2nd – not January 1st, that is our mid-winter) following on to the Spring. There will be days of frost when the sky is a clear pale blue the'colour of a duck's egg, and all things glisten silver and gold in the sun's first rays and the cold dry air makes one want to shout, and the vigour of work with saw or spade is itself a joy. There will be days of snow, when the earth will be muffled in white, and all the trees will carry white blossoms of snow on their branches and the sun when it comes will touch the whiteness to rose and gold and lay shadows of pure cobalt beyond every tree and in every hollow. There will be all the mornings when the cattle come down for their hay, black-red winter beasts, winter-hungry. Dark ice-cold mornings too, with bitter east winds when I must see the sheep at first light, and they will come running to me for their ration of 'cake'. There will be days when hounds are hunting on the hill and come screaming down into the combe below, and I shall take my stick and old field-glasses and go a-hunting too, called on and on by the flying crying pack and the oldest drama in the world, that of the hunter and the hunted.

There will be the days of rain and mud and lengthening evenings that lead on into Spring, then Spring itself! Days when the wild west wind rips the clouds apart and drives them galleon-like across a sky of electric-blue, and the smell of the sea mingles with the scent of the moor, of bog and burnt ground and earth and moss. Days when the first primroses peep from the banks and snowdrops and crocus appear in the garden and the buds swell on the trees. Days full of waiting, waiting … until one day you can smell the growing grass under your feet and see the sheen of green across the meadows. Spring is come, the Promise of Life that faileth never, and all the pent-up life that has slept in winter bursts forth in plant and beast and the heart of Man. Oh Spring, Goddess of Life, for whose coming we have all hungered in the long night of winter!

There will be days when all my daffies bloom again, and the narcissus too, in banks of yellow and white around the garden, and the birds sing all day and the sun is like a caress. Days when I work-down the fragrant-smelling soil, and set my first seeds, still with the awe as of a child, that these tiny brown things should turn into green and living plants. Days when the bronze-budded beech suddenly bursts into such a glory of green as no mortal mind could imagine of itself, translucent golden green like a million, million green butterflies trembling in the breeze. Days when the golden gorse floods its sun-warmed scent down all the hillsides and white lambs play on emerald grass amongst white daisies. Days when I shall go out into the garden, full of a curious intense excitement to see what of my seeds have come up in the night – and oh the wonder of those first tiny brave green seedlings – I know that I will kneel before them, physically to get a better look at them, yet also in an act of worship that is beyond all understanding. Days when the sou'west wind and the sun say 'come away, come away, over the hills and far away . . .' and I'll take my stick and sketching-things and fill my pocket with oatmeal and off I'll go exploring like an adventurer of old, climbing hills and wading rivers and striding over wide stretches of moorland high under the sky.

Then summer days will come, days when the sun grows hot and strong, when trees stretch out their boughs in canopies of heavy leaf and buttercups star the meadow grass. Days when the river runs glittering in its valley, a singing voice in the heat, and I can splash in its waters or sit on its banks amongst the flowery stands of water dropwort. Evenings when sunset mirrors on the surface and I can fish for trout. Then the hottest of hot days, when the heady, heavy scent of hay is over the fields, and we shall be 'carrying' again, with laughter and fun and tea in the corner of the meadow.

Days when I shall see friends from a distance again. Days when I pick my first green vegetables, and mow the lawn, and listen to the bees amongst the summer flowers. And just days when I walk among the foxgloves and young green bracken and look at butterflies and spiders' webs and tiny wonderful things at my feet.

Days when the corn stands golden unto harvest and I lift the frothy-headed oaten-sheaves in my arms again. Days when the heather is come, its purple glory spread across the hills, the soft wind blowing its scent to me, sweet and heady like a mixture of honey and wine in the sun. When I can crouch amongst its tussocks and look up at the sky through its bells of purple and amethyst and be half-intoxicated by its splendour.

Then autumn days when the valleys are veiled in mist at sunrise and woodsmoke hangs fragrant on the air at dusk. Days when I will pick blackberries and mushrooms again, and when painted toadstools will arise under the trees. Days when the fern will turn to sheets of copper and the beech to flame and the oaks to beaten gold, and I will be bewildered trying to catch the colours with my paintbox before the leaves come down for winter-time.

Days when I hunt the fields and copses, gun in hand, knowing the intensity of the hunter, the instinct old as time, the triumph of the kill, the satisfaction of meat in the pot.

Then the days that herald winter, shortening before the lengthening nights. Days that are half long evenings, with the cosy pleasure of log-fires, books and the radio to round them off, then lamp-lit working mornings to follow night.

So to winter again, then with God's grace another Spring beyond that. For all the days of life, I give thanks, Amen, Amen.

Conclusion

NOW I come to the end of this little book – or will have when I finish these last few pages. What shall I say in conclusion? Firstly, that when I set out to live as I have lived and do as I have done, I did so with no preconceived ideas or motives other than those expressed in the foregoing Introduction – to wit, to provide myself with the personal freedom and out-door life which was absolutely necessary to my well-being. I sought to prove nothing, only to live according to my natural urges.

Yet, looking back over those years of endeavour, it seems to me that I have discovered remarkable things and that I have proved something – though exactly *what* I am not myself quite certain.

Living close to Nature has taught me much, oh so much, in so many ways. I have learned, as set forth herein, the meaning of positive good health, and how this is linked directly with the soil. I have learned how health and happiness are themselves linked together, each conducive to the other, I have learned that freedom from frustration plus personal achievement are the roots of true happiness.

I have also come to the contemplation of deeper things and reached certain conclusions therefrom concerning the true values of life.

It seems to me, looking outwards, that this world has gone mad. All its standards are set on false values. Money is made the god of all. Success or failure, good or bad in life, are judged solely on whether money is made or not. For the sake of money, and the superfluous goods and enervating way of living that it brings, people shut themselves up in factories and offices away from the sunlight, to the end of covering the life-giving earth with concrete and tarmac, sending out more and more monstrous traffic and machinery to deaden their hearing and pollute the air, making cities to spread like a cancer full of crime and weariness, and binding themselves with the ties of frustration and ill-health.

Money as such is a useful invention, making commerce possible beyond the state of barter. A moderate amount is necessary to us all. But consider: of all the things you buy, that which you buy dearest of all is money. For money you sell the hours, the days of your life, which are the only true wealth you have. You sell the sunshine, the dawn and the dusk, the moon and the stars, the wind and the rain, the green fields and the flowers, the rivers and the sweet fresh air. You sell health and joy and freedom.

Industry likewise is a necessary thing in itself – all crafts are industries – to balance life. The gardener must have his spade, the hunter his ammunition, the artist his paints. (And without industry this little book would not be printed.) Town and country must balance each other. But they do not: industry has become an end in itself, an evil giant, eating up the goodness of life, despoiling the earth, feeding only to enlarge itself, deluding men that its material products will give them fullness of life.

It seems to me, these two things, money and industry, both so useful and necessary in themselves, have long passed the point of balance in life and are out of control, like a pair of bolting horses heading for a cliff-edge.

Instead of our controlling them, they now control us, and are taking us on to Hell.

I see this unrestrained cult-worship of money and material goods moving towards a terrible destruction of life: not only of the earth and physical well-being, but of moral and spiritual being. As men are besotted by the money and goods they worship, so they will do anything for these, and ethical values go overboard.

Again, consider, what are the true values of life? What is the good of fridges and freezers when there is less and less fresh food to put in them?

What is the good of cars bought for holidaying when there is nowhere to go in them because industry and the motorways are decimating the countryside?

What is the good of fancy furnishings and colour T.V. indoors when crime proliferates in the streets outside?

What is the good of an educational system wherein youngsters are trained in many things, all materialistic, but are not taught to speak the truth, respect the property of others or act with courtesy to fellow men?

What is the good of earning big money doing what you don't like and taking orders from somebody you hate, all for the sake of a fortnight's escapist holiday a year and the hope of a pension to eke out a frustrated old age?

Worst of all what is the good of doing something you are ashamed of to get big money, and having to live with shame in your heart for ever?

What avails an expensive health service (laudable though this is) when more and more people are becoming ill through unhealthy living?

What is the good of a Welfare State when it takes away a people's backbone and makes them subservient and utterly dependent on it?

What is the end for a world in which industry swallows up fresh air and earth and water, and all the beauty and fruitfulness of the earth to spew out endless plastic, concrete, tarmac, ironmongery, fumes, noise and ugliness?

What ultimately is the good of money when there is nothing worthwhile to spend it on?

For myself, I have tried to live an independent and balanced life within the means that I have had, according to my personal needs and moral beliefs, and these are the things I have found good and true: that one should hold first to ethical and moral principles, the highest that you know. That you should be true to yourself (else you will be true to no one) and that you should 'follow your Star' no matter how hard the path towards it. (You may not reach your goal, but to try is the greatest thing.) Work hard at whatever is your chosen work. Dare to take a calculated risk. Fight a good fight. Have courage and don't give way when things are hard and it would be easy to do so. Practise self-help – help yourself and help your neighbours. Give freely whatever you have to give to those around you. Deal honestly and honourably with all men. Above all, have faith – faith in whatever God you ultimately believe in.

As for my own way of life, I have done the best I can within the limits of what I could. If I had had more then I would have done more. I do not suggest that everyone should live their lives just as I live, or that it would be good for them or the country as a whole if they did so. It takes all sorts to make a world, and there must be captains and kings and hewers of wood and drawers of water, as the Good Book saith. What I do say, is that it would do most people good to live thuswise for a short period of their lives – say for one year – for this would, I am sure teach them oh so much about real life and its true values as to be of lasting benefit to them all the rest of their days.

Also I say, I feel that what I have learned may in some small way point to a better way of life, albeit on a different scale, for those folk who seek for an alternative to the fearful and self-destructive path of modern industrial-urban society which leads ever onwards to greed and ugliness and disaster, and death of the Spirit.

THE END

End Piece
Pictures and Places

End Piece
Pictures and Places